'This book should be essential reading for anyone doing business or even contemplating doing business in China. It gives concise and practical advice for negotiating the unique cultural hazards and logistical hurdles business-people face in this challenging but eternally alluring market. The real-life case studies, set in a lucidly presented social and historical context, are wonderfully entertaining and packed with valuable psychological insights.'

Susan R.S. Schofield, Executive Director, North Asia Region, American Express Bank

'*China Business* cuts through the myths surrounding trading with China and offers practical guidance on winning business as China's enterprise reform takes hold. Carolyn Blackman shines light on the issues important to business people developing strategies for the China market.'

Martin Walsh, Australian Trade Commission's Senior Trade Commissioner in Beijing

'Colourful, incisive, informative, down-to-earth, this book by Carolyn Blackman brings together the often hard-earned experience of many foreign companies working in China. The somewhat daunting challenge of reaching profitability in China is all too evident in the words of the managers and supervisors Carolyn Blackman has collected together for this very readable book. It should be a "required read" for those in foreign enterprises that wish to do, or are already doing, business in this great, rumbustious and intriguing country.'

Brian Anderson, Chairman, Shell Companies in North East Asia (China, Hong Kong, Taiwan, Korea)

'*China Business* is essential reading for anyone wanting to understand the hidden agendas when doing business in China. It reveals many of the tricks on how to succeed in China outside the negotiating room.'

Bill O'Shea, President, Australia China Business Council, Victoria Branch

'The direct style and quotations from extended frank interviews offer the reader a sense of a conversation and sharing of experience by people who have had to make it in business in China, often on the run, learning as they go. Many will recognise the situations and find illumination and help from Carolyn Blackman's analysis of the context. Newcomers to China will find it an easily accessible entrée to the challenges they are about to meet. A valuable addition to the China business library for those who want to learn about the experience and think about the implications.'

Stephen FitzGerald, Chairman, The Asia–Australia Institute

China Business

The rules of the game

Carolyn Blackman

ALLEN & UNWIN

First published in 2000

Allen & Unwin
83 Alexander Street
Crows Nest NSW 2065 Australia
Phone: (61 2) 8425 0100
Fax: (61 2) 9906 2218
E-mail: frontdesk@allen-unwin.com.au
Web: http://www.allenandunwin.com

National Library of Australia
Cataloguing-in-Publication entry:

Blackman, Carolyn.
   China business: the rules of the game.

   Bibliography.
   Includes index.
   ISBN 1 86508 230 9

   1. International business enterprises—China. 2. International business enterprises—China—Case studies. 3. Negotiation in business—China—Case studies. 5. Organizational change—China. 6. Success in business—China. I. Title.

338.70951

Set in 11/13pt Arrus by DOCUPRO, Sydney
Printed by Markono Print Media Pte Ltd, Singapore

10 9 8 7 6 5 4 3 2

Human beings are drawn close to one another by their common nature, but habits and customs keep them apart.

Confucius

I knew that the Chinese traditionally hold their table tennis bats the way we hold cigarettes. What I did not know was that they also hold their cigarettes the way we hold our table tennis bats.

Douglas Adams

Contents

Preface

This book began with the question, 'What is it like to operate a business in China?' The question came about when I was interviewing people for my book on negotiations in business in China. It was always difficult to keep my interview subjects to the strict topic of negotiations, as they would invariably want to talk about their other experiences in China: the Chinese business people and bureaucrats they had met, the banquets they'd attended, the factories they'd visited, the places they'd travelled to —everything that had preceded and followed the actual negotiations. I realised that there was a rich field here to explore and that the experiences of these business people were worth telling.

Thus I began to talk to all kinds of business people, from the CEOs of multinational companies and their managers in China, in operations and marketing, to the sole traders, sometimes operating on the edge of the law and certainly on their wits. My focus was on what happens after the negotiations.

I wanted to get close to the real experience of Western managers, of what it feels like to be operating within the Chinese context far from home. I didn't want an idealised portrait. I wanted the day-to-day experience as it is lived. I wanted to know what those generalisations—'relationships not law', 'joint venture partner conflict' or 'same bed, different dreams', a 'developing country' and 'management challenges'—meant for the individual Western executive. Each case study in this book documents a Western executive's thinking about his or her on-the-ground experience. It gives, as the Chinese say, 'skin and feathers' to the 'bones' of commercial reporting.

Each case study is followed by a commentary. This is a search for meaning in the interactions between Westerners and Chinese. I hope that, through both the case studies and the commentaries, those in business with the Chinese will find not only a light shone on their own experiences but also some insights into what accounts for these experiences and how we might fine-tune our response. My other aim was to document elements of the Chinese environment that seemed pertinent to Western managers in China, those things vaguely referred to as 'Chinese business culture'. I hope that the discussion will help Western business people to see more deeply into the workings of Chinese society.

I owe many debts for the help I have received while writing this book. My first debt is to the business people who gave of their time and thoughts. All were most generous in sharing their experiences, both good and bad, their achievements and their frustrations. Neither their names nor those of their companies have been used, so as to protect confidentiality.

The University of Ballarat funded part of the research and provided an invaluable library service that expedited my quest for international research and memoirs in this area. Sue Taylor and Carmel Grant helped me to access published material and on-line services.

I wish particularly to acknowledge my colleagues at the University of Ballarat, Dr Xiaoli Jiang and Ms Sari Baird, for many hours of interesting discussion on the Western–Asian business relationship. Dr Xiaoli Jiang gave me access to her own interview material which enlarged my understanding. She provided the interview on which the case study in Chapter 10 is based. Ms Sari Baird undertook the interview that forms the basis of the case

study in Chapter 12. I am grateful to other colleagues—
Irene Keating, Tanya Adair, Rosemary Green, John
Mcdonald, John Maguire and Koji Hoashi—for their
always cheerful response to my many requests.

In China I was helped in various ways by Martin
Walsh, Senior Trade Commissioner, Austrade, Beijing,
Richard Pillow, then Trade Commissioner, Shanghai and
Marc Gauci. Peter and Cathy Rogers of ECA Asia Pacific
in Melbourne gave me many opportunities to speak with
expatriates. They also offered most enjoyable hospitality
and informed discussion on cross-cultural business issues.
I was also fortunate to receive generous-spirited support
at critical times from Maura Fallon in Hong Kong and
George Renwick of Renwick & Associates, Carefree, Ari-
zona, USA. They shared their own rich experiences as
consultants, mediators and trainers in China. The members of the Australia China Business Council, especially
Tony Kosky, Bill O'Shea, Jane Orton and Barry White,
always brought me down to earth with their practical
approach to business dealings with the Chinese. My
gratitude is also due to Lawrence and Kathy Doolan, who
always offer lively discussion on a wide variety of issues
and a welcome in Melbourne. Finally, many thanks are
due to my husband, Wilson, who cheered me on daily
as the book was being written. As for the selection and
interpretation of the material, as many business people
say: 'The buck stops here.'

Carolyn Blackman
Ballarat, October 1999

Glossary

The pinyin version of Chinese characters is given first, followed by the Wade-Giles romanisation.

Changjiang	Yangtze
chop	official stamp of approval
da chi da he	literally 'big eating, big drinking'
ganbei	literally 'dry glass', a toast equivalent to 'bottoms up', 'cheers'
ganqing	emotional attachments, feelings
guanguanxianghu	bureaucrats shielding one another
guanxi	relationships, connections
Guomindang	Kuomintang
Hanjian	traitor to China
Hankou	Hankow
houtai laoban	backstage bosses
jinqian	money (ties)
juan, juanshu	contribution, subscription
kaoshan	supporters
kejuan zashui	exorbitant levies and sundry taxes
liyi	interest (ties)
maotai	sorghum-based spirit used for toasting

MOFTEC	Ministry of Foreign Trade and Economic Co-operation
nuoyong	literally 'shift and use', to divert funds, to misappropriate funds
shang xing, xia xiao	what the superior does, those below copy
Shanxi	Shansi
Sunzi	Sun Tzu, author of *The Art of War* and *The Thirty-six Stratagems*, a manual on strategy in warfare
tael	unit of currency used in early nineteenth-century China
tianzi	birth (ties)
tianzui	literally 'stuff the mouth', to silence a critic
tiao jiangguo	stir the gluepot
tongxianghui	associations of native place
yan jiu	to study, cigarettes and liquor
yiren dedao, jiquan shengtian	when a man attains the Tao, his chickens and dogs ascend with him to heaven
zhanguang	literally 'sharing in the light'
zhengdang	fair treatment

Introduction

On a beautiful autumn day in Beijing I accompanied a coffee importer, an expatriate, on his rounds to collect outstanding debts. We set off in his authentic Beijing Jeep—that fine example of Chinese socialist engineering. The chaotic traffic necessitated many gear changes and they were all rough. We visited numerous coffee bars, at all of which there was a long discussion with the owners: they would pay their accounts *if* he fixed their broken toilets, or *if* he provided and installed a new coffee machine, or . . . There was always an 'if . . . then . . . '. Most hadn't paid their bills in six months. In a couple of the coffee bars, we came across the representatives of big international beer companies who also were trying to extract what they'd been owed for six months.

On one occasion my friend emerged triumphantly from the discussion with a cheque, only to discover later that it had been back-dated. Chinese banks won't honour a cheque that is more than 30 days old, which meant that he would have to retrace his steps to that coffee bar and begin the negotiation anew. After a day spent in '*cherchez le cheque*', my coffee importer friend was no better off financially, and I had had my bones rattled to death by his old Jeep.

In this story we are face-to-face with some of the realities of China for Western expatriates. The Beijing Jeep symbolises the old Chinese technologies—outdated, poor in quality, a low level of engineering, and lacking in comfort; while the apparently Western-style coffee bars hide facets of contemporary commercial life in China—debt and ingenious ways to avoid payment.

Western executives have to deal with this complex and sometimes hostile environment as outsiders, usually without being able to speak and understand Chinese. Although many Western companies had the intention to replace their expatriate executives with locals, most now expect to have expatriates in China for years to come. Transferring technology and management systems from the West to China, and building market share, have turned out to be a longer-term process than expected.

One reason is that China is a developing country. A few indicators give some meaning to this description. Only 1.1 per cent of the population over 25 years of age has post-secondary school education (Kurain 1998). Internal transportation is not in the hands of the most efficient freight movers, the trucking companies, but is dominated by barges on the waterways and canals. (Forty-nine per cent of freight is moved by waterways, compared with 15.7 per cent by road, according to the *China Statistical Yearbook 1997*.) A wine and beer bottle factory which has to transport its bottles in hessian sacks on barges, and not in sturdy crates and cartons by door-to-door transport, consequently has a high breakage rate and slow delivery time. Risk due to poor infrastructure is high, and the unexpected often catches Western executives unprepared. Executives in a malting company which prepared hops for foreign beer brewers thought that the water tasted rather salty. At dinner with local officials the reason emerged by chance. Someone had made a hole in the main water pipes from the local reservoir, and the local water authorities had decided to make good the supply by diverting reprocessed water—with a high salinity level—from the Pearl River into the system. While dinner was proceeding, the boilers on which the local electricity supply depended exploded, cutting off electricity supplies. The entire hop malting was ruined and the machinery seriously damaged. The cost to the company was US$3 million.

Another influence on the rate of China's adoption of Western business ways is China's '4000 years of history'. Being such a self-contained civilisation, China has found solutions to the problems of human organisation and co-operation that are often different from those fashioned in the West. Even with the huge inrush of foreign investment and foreign companies since 1978, China's own internal economy is dominant. In 1996 the foreign investment share of GDP was 5 per cent, the share of gross domestic investment was 14 per cent and the share of industrial output was 14.5 per cent (*China Statistical Yearbook 1997*). It is natural, therefore, that Chinese commercial practices dominate the business environment.

Time and again, Western expatriates when in conflict with Chinese businesses have said to me, 'It's a waste of time to threaten legal action' or 'We've taken legal action, but it's useless because they don't care.' A Chinese friend who is well connected in the bureaucratic power structures said to me in disbelief and outrage one day, 'Mr Wang is suing my family! Doesn't he know our uncle is a magistrate?' Simon Lin, president of Taiwan's computer giant, ACER, crystallised the difference in official attitudes to business between the West and China in the matter of fair treatment. When he tells Chinese officials that fair treatment is necessary for him to invest, 'They accuse me of not trusting them,' he says. 'And sometimes they even threaten me.' After that they may just as easily turn around and offer him special arrangements, which he sees as a sign of trouble. In the West, his reference to fair treatment is accepted as simply his effort to control risk (Baum 1999). For Westerners working in this environment, there are obviously things about the legal system and the bureaucratic system that they need to know.

Expatriate managers are sent to China, willingly or unwillingly, to achieve certain goals. Once there, they find that neither their Chinese employees, nor the Chinese business operating environment, are copies of their equivalents at home. They must find their way by making accommodations and adjustments as they go.

Sometimes the stresses of such adjustments tell on expatriates and locals alike. A Chinese manager said of an expatriate responsible for technology transfer: 'This manager is extremely arrogant and insulting, and shows no respect for the Chinese people. His attitude is probably due to his time in Nigeria, where he was used to beating up and scolding blacks. We are different, because we are not used to being subjugated under any colonial power, and we have a long cultural history.' (Hoon-Halbauer 1996, p. 143)

It may be that the expatriate manager was driven to be dictatorial by the situation. He had to achieve corporate goals devised remote from Chinese realities in his company's European head office, and he was faced with Chinese incapacity to respond appropriately. It is obvious, however, that the Chinese employees had their own point of view and their co-operation was not a foregone conclusion. It is all very well to have a strategic plan, but it is individuals who must realise it and do so in a context that is imperfect, changing and alien. It is all these aspects of doing business in China—'the rules of the game' in regard to relations with employees, the business infrastructure and the role of the bureaucracy in business—that this book describes.

The heart of this book lies in the case studies. These draw on a wealth of experience and insights gained by Western executives in China. Each case details the lessons executives have learned and gives a candid portrait of the Chinese business environment and its unwritten rules.

I have tried throughout to let Western executives speak for themselves, since they are the ones daily facing the Chinese context and grappling with its challenges. What they do and say may not follow orthodox Western practice, but this is one of the realities of 'think global, act local'. After each study is a commentary which explains the main issues, places them in a broader context and provides useful strategies. The reader should gain an understanding of what it is really like to be a Western expatriate manager in China, of the idiosyncrasies of the Chinese environment and of why expatriates use the strategies they do. The reader should thus acquire a framework for dealing with China which leads to greater understanding and effective outcomes.

I hope that this book will do what many companies fail to do for their expatriates entering China: to pass on information about the valuable lessons learned by previous expatriates. I also hope that the discussion will open up the rationale of some essentially 'Chinese' business characteristics. China represents a significant cultural and economic entity in the global context, and it is worthwhile for Western managers and policy-makers to know more about it and how things function there.

Part I of the book examines some of the major themes of the case studies: customary Chinese business practices, networking, competition, corruption and communication. It looks at these themes from both a Western and a Chinese perspective and documents how consistent they have been in the Chinese business environment. Each chapter in Part 1 sets out significant 'ground rules' that Western executives in China need to address.

Part II provides an insight into how four successful companies in their home markets and in other Western markets have experienced China. The four case studies are told from the point of view of the head office executives responsible for China operations. Chapter 5 addresses the market, Chapter 6 the relationship between partners in a joint venture, Chapter 7 ethical challenges, and Chapter 8 the limits of trust.

Part III focuses on the day-to-day management experiences of five foreign executives in manufacturing joint ventures. In Chapter 9 the managing director discusses his relationship with the Chinese directors, their different agendas and expectations. In Chapter 10 two young operations managers explain their control problems. In

Chapters 11, 12 and 13, executives trace how their experiences delegating duties to Chinese staff have changed the way they manage in China.

Part IV addresses a feature of the Chinese business landscape that differs significantly from most Western countries: the power of the bureaucracy. Examples show how the bureaucracy at central and local levels relates to Western and local Chinese businesses. Local Chinese business people illuminate the expectations, interrelationships and normal functioning of the government bureaus in a purely Chinese context. Western business people give their strategies for dealing with this specifically Chinese feature. Chapter 14 discusses the meaning of 'socialist market' characteristics and central law-making. Chapter 15 gives examples of how local governments impose additional taxes on foreign-invested businesses, and Chapter 16 illustrates the multiplicity of taxing bureaus and the unwritten rules for dealing with their impositions. In Chapter 17, local Chinese business people disclose some of their strategies in relation to bureau officials, and a Western executive shares his success with the local power-holders. In Chapter 18, executives discuss what they have learned about dealing with Chinese bureaucrats.

In the conclusion the patterns of the Chinese business environment and Western perspectives are brought together. The bibliography gives details of many books and articles of interest to business people, international business students and the general public.

The Chinese like to use the word 'pragmatic'. By this I think they mean facing and dealing with reality, as opposed to following rhetoric or written rules. I like to think that this book, in the best Chinese tradition, is 'pragmatic'.

Quick reference chart to aspects of the Chinese business scene

Aspect	Chinese background	strategy	chapter number
Banquets and entertainment: • challenges in toasting and food • strength as an influence strategy	• Group nature of Chinese society: participatory, fun activity • Bonding mechanism in hierarchical, structured and formal relationships • Freedom to talk 'off the record' • Influence mechanism: host's 'face' lifted by lavish hospitality	• Toasting: invite the group to join in, bring your own support group • Be aware that important issues can be brought up unexpectedly • Learn a few good songs for the karaoke: join in! • Use banquet/ hospitality as an influence strategy	1, 16
Distribution: • localised • Chinese monopoly • highly competitive • questionable ethics	• Socialist period: territorial monopolies, multiple levels • Inadequate transport systems across provinces • Past emphasis on quantity, not quality and brand names	• Key to sales • Devote time to logistics • Maintain brand name control • Seek out and test many distributors • Avoid 'exclusive agency' distributors • Use 'If . . . then . . .' negotiation strategy	1, 9
Sub-contracting: • pyramid, small margins • localisation policy	• Traditional collusive practices through guilds/chambers of commerce • Tradition of 'the squeeze'/personal margin • Socialist hierarchical monopolist system	• Seek out private contractors • Have a direct relationship	1
Sharp practices	• Highly competitive environment: few resources, many people • Customary distance of government from business–business contract enforcement	• Beware: whenever there is an opportunity for personal benefit it is likely to be taken • Question everything, be circumspect	1, 5, 10

Quick reference (continued)

Aspect	Chinese background	strategy	chapter number
Sharp practices (cont.)	• Explosion of the market since the opening-up: greed! • Haggling tradition, inflated prices • Different ethical tradition: *Sunzi* and deception strategy for strategic advantage • Customary use of deception as a business tactic with strangers • Pressure of corporatisation of government departments, profit motive leads to short-term focus	• Check it out yourself • Be prepared to bargain • Keep cool	
Competition: • local businesses • government support and protection for local businesses • excess capacity • international competition • counterfeiting, smuggling	• Poor country, limited purchasing power • Similar to the Western business experience in China from 1850–1950s • Small commissions between Chinese traders • Higher cost of foreign goods: expat salaries, higher Chinese salaries • Weak compliance mechanisms	• Use and control brand names/brand strength associated with quality, reliability, service • Negotiate local government support/protection • Localise staff: lower salary and benefit costs • Counterfeiting: court action or use 'Chinese' direct methods of control	2, 5
Corruption: • officials • nepotism • patronage	• 'Family-first' ethics • 'Sharing in the light': reciprocity and group benefits • 'Entrusted' or 'inherent' power of officials—control over licences, permits, land etc.	• Cultivate relations with bureaucrats, but be aware of corruption laws • Be aware of the customary expectation of a 'personal margin'	3, 5, 7, 10

Quick reference (continued)

Aspect	Chinese background	strategy	chapter number
Corruption (cont.) • 'squeeze', extortion • bribery	• Personal morality as controlling mechanism, poor compliance mechanisms • Low official salaries • 'Those below copy those above': *shang xing xia xiao*	• Have a strategy • Use 'government co-ordination department'/ go-betweens • Use Public Security Bureau in petty crime	
Communication: • indirect • incomplete • status influence in boss–subordinate • information as power • problems disguised • unpredictable 'face' issues • misleading • 'white lies' • misinterpretation	• High context affects argument style, meetings, negotiation styles • Status: boss in charge of penalties and rewards; respect leads to 'good news stories' • Hierarchical system: information as power • 'Conceptual' communication, gap in experiences • Insider–outsider difference in ethical standards • Group effect: maintenance of face before peers • Pragmatic business ethics based on strategic advantage (*Sunzi*—the Art of War)	• Listen closely • Spend time communicating • Wait for recommendations in the tail • Be aware of status effects on subordinate communication with the boss • Demonstrate what you want • Use group problem-solving without superiors • Avoid confrontation unless calculated, go sideways, show flexibility • Control immediate responses, think long term • Think about behind-the-scenes scenarios • Have trustworthy lieutenants • Beware of the difficulty of interpreting correctly • Pay attention to interpreter's needs, interests and loyalty • Train staff in English	4, 5, 12, 13

Quick reference (continued)

Aspect	Chinese background	strategy	chapter number
Contract defaulting	• Highly competitive market • Lots of bad practice • Inadequate enforcement mechanisms–tradition of hands-off government in commercial litigation • Agreements not do-able due to debt, corporatisation, withdrawal of government support	• Careful risk assessment • Use *guanxi* pressure • Build-in penalties • Negotiate, renegotiate	5, 6
Debt	• Triangular debt • Lack of enforcement mechanisms • State-owned enterprises non-profitable, social welfare responsibilities • Debt collection agencies illegal • Traditional long credit terms	• Use a 'no credit' policy • Payment before supply • Payment before next supply • Find trade offs, flexibility in means of payment • Use 'ultimate consequences' negotiating tactic • *Guanxi* pressure	5, 7
Honesty and deception, 'white lies'	• Financial and political imperatives • Insider–outsider distinctions: low trust in outsiders • Deception for strategic advantage ethically okay: pragmatism • 'Losing face': public embarrassment unacceptable • Historical mistrust of foreign business	• Look for underlying truths • Keep calm • Use individual interviews, go behind the scenes • Watch for indirect communication • Build trust	8, 10

Quick reference (continued)

Aspect	Chinese background	strategy	chapter number
Joint venture shared management:	• Local priorities: communist background of directors, managers; external pressures	• Gain management dominance • Convert to wholly-owned enterprise • Limit number of Chinese board members	6, 8, 9
• different/ hidden agendas, expectations, priorities • power struggles • dishonesty, aggressive attacks • exclusion of expatriates	• Co-operation and trust undermined by poor business performance • Chinese unfamiliar with Western business priorities (e.g. reinvestment) • Joint venture management problems a common phenomenon in joint ventures all over the world		
Workplace culture change:	• Socialist enterprise culture: based on command economy and political control	• Greenfield site • Recruit young staff • Train, train, train • Western manager as coach • Implement clear and accountable systems	10, 11, 12, 13
• lack of quality focus • lack of customer focus • low skill levels/lack of exposure to high technology • undisciplined approach • command and control method: different concept of 'leadership'	• Only 1.1 per cent of population aged over 25 years with post-secondary education • Old networks of power: leadership based on age and seniority • Chinese 'slave characteristics': following orders	• Financial penalties and rewards • English language training • Small groups as focus • Support and shielding for middle managers • Advance slowly, maintain stability	

Quick reference (continued)

Aspect	Chinese background	strategy	chapter number
Supervisory–subordinate relationships: • status counts: fear and respect • staff wait on instructions • minor decisions referred upwards • abuse of 'democratic' management models • distrust of young expatriate managers • cliques • interpreter as go-between	• Traditional relationship: hierarchical, directive, punitive • Model of benevolent but strict official: 'mother and father' to the people • 'Sharing in the light' (*zhanguang*) and benevolence towards subordinates • Decision-making confined to top level • Reporting upwards and meetings affected by status • Weakness in producing pros/cons: educational outcomes from modelling education	• Show strength • Institute accountability systems • Financial penalties and rewards • High ratio of supervisory staff to worker • Maximise use of experienced management staff • Key aim: 'enable staff to get the job done' • Build trust through modelling, socialising, banquets • Be aware of staff feelings: be indirect • Educate head office	10, 11, 12, 13
Top-down legislation: • sudden changes • lack of consultation with business • lack of enforcement across all businesses	• State-controlled economy in socialist period • Rapidly moving economy and infrastructure development • Poor enforcement mechanisms	• Join with other foreign businesses in pressure group • Use diplomatic/commercial representatives • Use chambers of commerce	14
Central–local differences in legislation	• 'Inherent' or 'entrusted' power of officials • Concept of central broad policy with 'concrete local conditions and actual needs'	• Negotiate • Realise the importance of local officials and bureaus • Keep good relationships: be hospitable	15

Quick reference (continued)

Aspect	Chinese background	strategy	chapter number
Central–local differences in legislation (cont.)	• National taxes levied locally • Enterprises as 'social units' for taxation and social policy: traditional group identification • Strong local loyalties: 'law of avoidance'		
Overlapping jurisdictions of local bureaus: • taxation • fines • regulation	• Taxing authority from central government • Financial distress of local bureaus • Socialist taxation through enterprises • Large increase in local functionaries • See foreign-invested businesses as wealthy	• Negotiate down • Give small perks e.g. lunch, banquet	16
Retrospective, excessive, ad hoc taxation	• Unequal power distribution between officials and public • Tradition of local 'tax bullies' • Transparent accounting gives opportunities for taxation: avoided by local businesses	• Negotiate on 'reasonableness' and 'fairness' not on 'law' • Keep good relationships and contacts	16
Local official-business relationships: • regular interference	• Socialist period enterprises run by bureaucrats • Lack of commercial legal infrastructure • 'Inherent' power of officials	• Foster relationships: banquets, perks • Give fee-for-service • Beware of corruption • Employ go-betweens with status/connections	16, 17

Quick reference (continued)

Aspect	Chinese background	strategy	chapter number
Local official-business relationships: (cont.) • control of many business inputs • official protection and extortion • official control of licences, utilities, land, transport, customs	• Large local bureaucracies • Long tradition of official participation in business		
Nature of bureaucrats: • risk-averse • slow • hidden decision-makers • status-conscious • detail-minded • little proactive communication, feedback	• Hierarchical system, punishment for erring in decision-making • Decisions made at the top • Rule books, internal regulations • Personalised bureaucracy • Large bureaucratic staff: attention to detail and exactness	• Allow time • Keep up relationships • Think through their personal and departmental needs • Be proactive • Learn the correct system, know the unwritten rules • Talk to other foreign executives • Be aware of status of bureaucrats: give respect • Examine your own attitude and approach	18

I

The Chinese face of globalisation

1

A lot to learn: 'Nowhere else in the world is it like this!'

An executive who has only a passing acquaintance with China, if any, might say, 'Well, we are all human beings underneath', with the implication that there is very little that is different about the Chinese and about doing business in China, and therefore little to learn beyond how to present one's business card politely and how to *ganbei* (make toasts) at a banquet. Let us start with the banquet and see if that is the case.

Banquets

There is a certain formality about banquets in China. Everyone sits in an anteroom first; if you are the honoured guest you will be seated next to the most important people, with others ranked around according to the hierarchy. Tea is served. After ten minutes of chit-chat, everyone gets up and walks into the banquet, which is usually held in a private room. The honoured guest sits facing the door.

There might be fifteen courses, and there will be *maotai*: the host makes a toast, and then you respond with a toast. As the banquet proceeds, you start to notice that some people are becoming very raucous. They are mixing scotch and other wines together. They are obviously set on drinking a lot of *maotai*, releasing their inhibitions and having fun. So far, so good. I will now let one executive tell of his experience.

'Once they said, "We are bringing along Mr X. He is the big boss man of the corporation. He's a great drinker, a really big, big drinker." They kept saying what a great drinker he was, how he could drink everyone under the table. I thought, "No way, fellas. I'll show you how it's done."

'When we got to the banquet, the "great drinker" turned out to be about five feet [152 centimetres] tall, seven stone [45 kilograms], and twenty years older than I was. I thought there was no way he could beat me, given my body weight and experience in drinking. I soon learned how he got a reputation for being a good drinker: he would have his minions toast the guest one by one, so that the guest would have to drink after each toast. When someone at the other end of the table stood up and said, "Mr Mitchell, I welcome you to our country. *Ganbei*", I replied, "No, I can't drink with just one of you. I always drink with *all* my friends". So, for every toast that individuals proposed to me, I insisted that everyone join in.

'After six or eight *maotais*, I took control. I'd fill my glass, then say to the boss man: "Thank you for such a magnificent meal. I would like you *all* to drink with me." Then a few minutes later I'd get back to it. So I made the running and made him knock off . . . I thought, "Now I've got you where I want you". After another eight *maotais*, I worked on him one-on-one, until I got him to the stage where he was a write-off. Then I stopped. Everyone knew that their great man hadn't won. After that I got one hell of a lot of respect, because I had taken him on and they knew I'd worked out their procedures and beaten them at their own game. Then you get a lot of respect . . . You see it in their body language and attitude.

'You need to show you're not a dumb Westerner. They had set up the competition by talking about their boss being such a great drinker. I couldn't have cared less, but they kept emphasising this, as if they were throwing out a challenge. If you walk into their trap and you do it their way and don't win, basically you are down-graded in their eyes. If you avoid the challenge altogether, you'll lose their respect. By working out how they do it, and winning, you get a lot of kudos. They think, "This guy's got standing. He's smart".'

The toasting isn't the only challenge this executive has to deal with. Another is food.

'They serve up all kinds of food. I've eaten rice sparrows. The sparrows eat the grains of rice at the rice harvest. They puff up and can't fly. The farmers net them and drop them, as they are—feathers, beak and all—into boiling oil. They come out like black squash balls. You chew the whole lot up. The Shanghai fairy crab is another special dish. First they'll have the big white worms you dig up from the sand. Then they bring on the crabs. Once in Shanghai I was sitting next to a Chinese lady engineer. She picked up the crab, pulled its feet off and twisted the top shell off the bottom shell and sucked up the meat, roe and everything. They serve tortoise in its shell. They take the lid off and you tear into it with your chopsticks. Snake, duck feet, chicken feet, pig intestines chopped and fried in chilli . . . '

At banquets, other kinds of challenges will occur. Here is another executive's experience.

'The whole thing is about losing face. Any relationship is built on a succession of challenges: whether you are doing business, are at a banquet or with a friend. Everything is based on challenging the next person. At a banquet there are various targets. The banquet lasts about four or five hours. The first impression that you have is that they are as keen as you are to have a good time. But it's not as simple as that. They are keen to have a banquet, because they have been through very hard times—that's human. But the various targets might be to extract information from people, test their reputation, test their endurance. Because in a banquet, basically, you drink a lot. First you are going to see who will still be standing up at the end. In a negotiation various parties are present, and at the banquet it might be appropriate for one party to be extinguished half-way through the banquet so that the other parties can talk more freely.

'I have been at banquets where not-so-desirable parties have been targeted and extinguished—in fact, once it was a political bureau. I've been in situations where it was quite clear that I was the party that had to be extinguished, and I had to fight. There were 30 people around the table, and you learn very quickly that each party is represented by three or four persons. If you have 26 other people consistently challenging three or four persons for three or four hours, you know who is on the hot spot. That's the name of the game. It is put in a way where the people who are consistently being chal- lenged are presented as the most important ones at the table. They have the highest grade in some kind of hierarchy. You might start to feel you are important, but as they consistently challenge you, you may end up with your head in your rice-bowl. That's when you work out that the predominant feeling around the table wasn't friendliness and hospitality, but the opposite!

'You can't say, "I can't drink today because I'm sick and I've got a liver condition". You have to cope with all that. If you are in the countryside, they drink three times as much as in the city. At every banquet they will bring a challenge foodwise. The dish is presented to you first. Nobody else is touching it. You've got to go through it first and guess what it is—and some items are very disgusting by our standards. But you eat what you are served. If you say, "I just can't", they'll say, "Well this guy isn't serious. He doesn't want to understand us". A lot of people will think you are an easy target, that you don't want to go all the way. So—scorpions, dog, monkey, eggs that have been in the ground for three years—these are the things you have to eat.'

After the banquet there may be karaoke. Everyone is

expected to sing. It means you are playing the game. This is a manifestation of a collectivist society where people are expected to put group participation and solidarity before individual preferences. The host, to show his status as a generous host and his regard for the enjoyment of his guests, may provide call girls. They will be available to pour the wine, share jokes and for more intimate entertainments later in the night.

For the Chinese, what matters is the toasting, the game playing and what issues can be resolved 'between the meat and the wine'. Some Westerners eventually dispense with the banquet because they feel that in certain cases it's just an excuse for their Chinese associates to eat well and have a good time. Others use it to invite both the important people and their minions—the drivers, delivery people, the junior clerk, the multiplicity of underlings. In this way they get co-operation from all the people who might have an influence on their business dealings with the boss. Learning to pick the game that's being played is important to a foreign business person's sense of ease and, in this linguistically and culturally different environment, his or her degree of control.

Distribution and Chinese consumers

In strictly commercial matters, Western executives soon find that the distribution system in China is an area of intense and rapid learning. They might have assumed that the distribution system would be as straightforward as that in the advanced Western economies. But instead, they have had to grapple with the old state system where huge distributors appointed by the government had monopolies over their geographical area, and a hidden commission system with a vast network of lower-tier distributors. Chinese distributors are used to dealing with large quantities of product and a high wastage rate, so protecting quality products is entirely new to them.

Executives with an international beer manufacturing company had not anticipated this situation:

'At home we have computer on-line ordering systems. Our customers can fill out what they want, it's put on a truck and sent out. Here you have to buy the distribution by providing the right incentives. In Shanghai we started with 500 distributors. We found that they would try to deal us down a few cents and shave the margins. We gave various bonuses to distributors if they sold certain volumes. We set targets for them, but once they'd reached the target they sold off excess volume to other distributors. We gained nothing out of it except to understand that these people traded with one another for very small margins.'

The company has had to reduce the number of distributors they deal with, without really knowing the relationships between them. They had to get to know the distributors so that they could choose those who showed some loyalty and would look after the product.

'A normal distributor has a shed, ten crates high, six different brands. With the beer business being so competitive they are always undercutting one another and trying to kill off a competitor, and that affects the price initially and later on your stock. They don't have a lot of loyalty.

'They have a very high selling season in summer, so they will stock a product leading up to summer. We have bad weather in Shanghai leading up to summer, called the plum rains. If the product isn't in a good environment it will get wet, and mould and frost will damage it. If they leave it out in the sun, it gets damaged. So we try to pick people who will look after the product well.

'We deliver by truck and sometimes tricycle. There are transportation restrictions. You can't bring trucks into some areas; other areas you can't bring vans into. You have to double up your vehicles. You can't use your vehicle that ends in an even number on Tuesdays; you can only use the odd numberplate. It has to have a day off, or go to another part of the city. That is a logistical problem that takes time to understand. All distributors deliver by tricycle. The beer bottles can get broken, as they are moved four or five times from place to place. It goes from us to a distributor, to a second-tier distributor, then to the retail outlet. There are more steps in the process. Most of our product will be purchased at a little corner store, one or two crates by tricycle going to each of those, rather than one truck going to a supermarket.'

Learning how to market the product to local consumers engaged foreign executives in a step-by-step search to understand the consumers' values and beliefs.

'At the current time, Chinese consumers don't have loyalty to a particular brand. You don't just say, "This guy's a Budweiser drinker". Tomorrow he's a Bex drinker and the day after, Foster's—whatever is going. Our brand is bought by office workers, and occasionally by lower-income people who, when they go out once a month, maybe will buy a higher-priced product for relatives and friends, or for business reasons.

'Something else our company has to understand about the market is that there is a different way of consuming the product. Chinese people don't go to a bar and have a drink with friends. They drink at restaurants and banquets. They buy a higher-priced product to gain "face". They don't buy a local Guangming or Shanghai beer to entertain their father-in-law or best friend. To show them they are prospering, they would buy a foreign brand. A Guangming is for taking home and drinking on your own.

'The Chinese have strong views on maintaining an internal body heat. In summer they have watermelon to cool down; in winter they want to heat up, so they drink a different product to warm themselves up internally. Head office asks us: "Why is the market suddenly dropping off? Why can't we keep a steady sales going? Nowhere else in the world is it like this!" We say, "Well, in winter it's too cold". They reply, "Well, why don't people go someplace warm?". We say, "There aren't any warm places, but the time is coming when there will be". People go to better restaurants which are air-conditioned and they have a Mongolian hotpot. Then they want to cool down. So they think, "What will I have? I'll have a beer". They are balancing themselves all the time. In our home market, people go to a bar and drink. They don't eat anything, and they don't worry about the weather.

'The reasons that people buy beer are different for different products. You try to pick the mark. Where is the best place for you to put your effort? We have 60 to 70 sales and promotion girls who introduce the product to consumers. It's an effective way of getting our product through, especially to big restaurants such as a seafood restaurant with 100 tables doing 100 cartons a week. Sometimes the girls are just a walking billboard, so they may not always be selling beer. Sometimes they will be talking to consumers. Just so long as they are in the restaurant and not out the back sleeping!'

Expecting an open distribution system like the one they were used to in the developed Western countries, these executives had to spend time learning, by trial and error, about the interconnections between distributors, their motivations and their characteristics. Shanghai city's restrictions on vehicle use required a refiguring of the logistics system. Nor did Shanghai consumers follow the pattern of drinkers overseas. The foreign executives discovered that Chinese consumers have their own value and status systems, their own beliefs that affect the way they drink beer. A foreign beer gives them 'face'. It signals that they are prospering. Their belief in maintaining a constant body temperature is a decisive factor in when they drink beer. Just the lack of air-conditioning systems for the mass of Chinese people is a factor in sales growth.

You can hear the frustration in the words of the head office executive when he asked, 'Why is the market suddenly dropping off? Why can't we keep a steady sales going? Nowhere else in the world is it like this!'

Sub-contracting

In the construction industry, Western executives found that a system of sub-contracting banned in their home market was the normal system in China. Through pyramid sub-contracting, profits are shared by a large number of related groups. It follows the same pattern as the beer executives found among their distributors—that there was a monopoly structure and a lot of cross-trading for very small margins.

'There is a lot of pyramid sub-contracting. This is forbidden in many Western countries. You let the project to party A, party A lets it to party B, and party B lets it to party C . . . and D. So the person who is actually doing the work is at least three steps removed from the person you are paying, and all of these people are taking a cut off the top. So the contractor actually doing the work is getting one-quarter of what he should be getting, and hasn't been told about quality. He arrives on site and says, "Nobody told me I had to use extra special concrete. Nobody told me I had to make sure that the bars and reinforcing are inspected . . . "

'So we then dealt with the people we contracted and said, "This isn't good enough. It's not working properly. You've got to do something about it". They told their managers, who said: "This is China. Why is this job so special?" And the managers would tell the person who was actually doing the work. This bottom-level contractor probably had no idea about what he was being told because he wasn't familiar with our quality standards, so he didn't follow the specifications passed on by the Chinese manager.

'We stopped dealing through the chain of contractors. We worked directly with the workers themselves, showing them how to do the project. This upset people in the contracting chain. The middle managers said, "You are interfering with our work". We said, "Well, we did try and work through you".

'We are now dealing with the boss and owner of the

smaller contracting organisation. He has five of his brothers and friends working with him. Maybe he pays them
by piece-work, but he owns the company and he is
learning from us. It has probably offended all the other
contractors and sub-contractors, but I think there is an
understanding that we will deal this way unless we can
get the quality we want through doing it their way.'

Sharp practices

It is absolutely crucial in China to learn how to recognise
and deal with 'sharp practices'. Of course, people in
business anywhere in the world must be aware of sharp
practices. However, in China, because Westerners are
outsiders without the contacts they would have in their
own business context, they are more open to being
cheated. China's business environment is highly competitive. There are a lot of Chinese people struggling for a
share of the available resources and opportunities. There
is also the traditional philosophy of Sunzi who advocated
cunning as a prime tactic in warfare and, by extension,
business. The Chinese attitude is 'buyer—or investor—
beware'.

It has been a long tradition for the government to
have little to do with the implementation of commercial
regulations and dispensing justice in conflict resolution.
If commercial litigation was brought to a provincial court,
the litigants were expected to enforce the judgment themselves, and the court expenses were heavily against the
plaintiff. Some would say this tradition is alive and well
in contemporary China.

Some say that the prevalence of sharp practices is
largely the result of the marketisation of the economy.
This does play a part, but anyone who reads the accounts
of Westerners who did business with China before the
socialist market economy was instituted will be convinced
that sharp practices have long flourished in China and
that Western business people have always had to acknow-

ledge this as a feature of the Chinese commercial world and deal with it. In contemporary China, sharp practices pop up in the most unexpected places, as the following executives discovered. The first is from an executive who wished to buy land for a new factory in southern China.

'There are some very cunning people. I found that where they have a hill, they bring in a back-hoe to split it, putting the soil into the paddy. They end up with 30 hectares of flat land. If you're not smart you'll be sold 20 metres of uncompacted fill sitting on paddy or banana plantation. Two years later it is three metres lower than when you bought it, and if you want to build a factory, you've got to pile down 30 metres to get to firm ground. I would go around the outskirts of this industrial land they were trying to sell, and I could see where the bulldozer had pushed the dirt to the edge and it had fallen away. In the end, I bought our land where the base of the hill had been.'

The second example is from an architectural company. The company had excellent working relationships with Taiwanese clients and one of these clients referred them to a Shanghai developer. The developer proposed that they co-operate in building a golf club, shopping centres, 40-storey office towers and so on. In Shanghai the company executives searched for information about the client and the market. The information they were given turned out to be 'inaccurate, misleading and intentionally given to mislead'. The Shanghai design institutes 'convincingly indicated that they could be relied on for support', which the foreign executives later found was a way of 'lulling potential competition into a false sense of security, thereby gaining control over the potential competition'. The design institutes told the foreign architectural company what fees they were charging, but overstated them by 60 per cent, hoping that the foreign company would then quote too high and lose the project to the design institutes.

They also discovered that the Chinese developer only wanted them for the initial design concept. Once the contract had been signed the developer planned to hand over the documentation and detail to 'more or less anyone', leaving the architectural company with no control over quality in design or detailing—upon which they had built their reputation. In the joint venture discussion the Chinese developer omitted to mention that his construction companies were getting the contracts for the projects, a professional problem that should have been known to all parties. The Western firm withdrew, in time, and was later able to partner with another more suitable Chinese company.

The third example is from two young foreign technicians working in a factory in Tianjin.

'Sometimes we have ten jobs wanted on the one day, so we have to sub-contract out. The sub-contractors are found by the Chinese. When we send it out to a sub-contractor, the Chinese managers, who know how much it costs us, tell the sub-contractor it costs us 50 RMB [Renminbi]. So the sub-contractor puts in a quote for 40 RMB. But really it's only going to cost him 10 or 20 RMB. It's a free sort of market.

'When they give us the invoices, we go through them and take a third off every price, saying that's all that we'll pay. They don't even respond. It makes you wonder what the real profits are. The trouble is that they are all in it together. When we go back home and people try to swindle us, we'll be so experienced we'll say: "You don't even know where to start, boy!"'

These young technicians weren't used to the Chinese practice of submitting inflated invoices when they first arrived in China, but they quickly learned how to deal with it—to an extent. Their final comment expresses their shock at their new environment and at how different it is from their home environment.

Comment

People are unable to start doing business in China as if they were in the developed West. A business person must learn how the local scene works and then decide to what extent he or she will adapt to local ways. Obviously, they will have to participate in the banqueting rituals—the toasting, the eating, the game playing, the karaoke—but not necessarily the late-night hostess entertainment. Self-protection is necessary in the serious toasting. The executive's insistence that all his 'friends' share in those toasts directed exclusively at himself is a good strategy. It accepts the local custom, but it does not put him at a disadvantage. Duty is seen to be done, and the rules are accorded with.

The challenges of distribution and contracting were met by our Western executives in a similar manner: they found out how the local system worked and then tried to find ways around it. In this they are advantaged by the opening up of the Chinese economy to private enterprise.

For the beer manufacturer there was no way around taking the local customer values into account—their lack of loyalty to any particular foreign brand, the appeal of foreign beer to better-paid office workers, its use as a demonstration that they were doing well, of 'face', and the belief in balancing body heat.

In the matter of sharp practices, most Westerners learn through experience to be less trusting, to acknowledge the limits of government regulation and compliance mechanisms, and to expect that they are not always told the whole truth and nothing but the truth. Questioning everything is a strategy well worth learning.

2

Sustaining competitive advantage

A Western executive, reflecting on his experiences in China, said: 'Assume it is going to be hard, and then put a model together that says it is going to be harder than that. You've got to think through how quickly your product can be replicated by Chinese competitors. How sustainable is your competitive advantage? If I were starting again, I would be far more pessimistic about financial assumptions and profit assumptions, and about Chinese competitive behaviour. For a period there was an assumption that foreign companies would put their stamp on the market. I think they underestimated the ingenuity of the Chinese to engineer their own solutions to particular market requirements, or to copy very quickly the better ideas or access their technology directly through technology transfer agreements and then become straight-out competitors.'

A company which found its competitive advantages gradually moving to Chinese companies noted first that its sub-contractors had begun to use the same equipment. Chinese managers had been stealing the equipment and selling it to other organisations associated with the parent company. They sold drills worth 2000 RMB for 500 RMB and a 10 per cent kickback. The Chinese manager earned his monthly wage from selling one or two drills, and the sub-contractor gained top-quality tools for a quarter of the regular price. It was a satisfactory outcome for everyone except the foreign company.

Competing with the Chinese in China has always been an issue for foreign business. In 1878, Thomas Knox, an American merchant, observed: 'The result of this association of the foreigner and the Chinese in business has been not altogether to the advantage of the foreigner. The Chinese . . . has learned the lesson which the foreigner has unintentionally taught him, and learned it well. He . . . is proving more than a match for his instructor. In all the Chinese ports there are Chinese banks, Chinese insurance companies, Chinese boards of trade, Chinese steamship companies . . . all in Chinese management, and supported by Chinese capital.' (Hao 1970, p. 117)

Another American, Augustine Heard, Jr, wrote about the trade between Chinese ports and other Asian ports: 'Formerly this was all in the hands of foreigners, but as the Chinese grew to understand foreign methods, they took it themselves, and why should they not? They were as clever as other merchants; they could get advances from the Banks; they could use the telegraph, and above all, they paid no commission or brokerage in China, which the foreigner must do.' (Hao 1970, p. 117)

An advantage which Chinese businesses have is their lower costs. Their products may be 30 per cent cheaper than a foreign company's, even though the foreign company's prices might be 30 per cent below global prices. In contemporary China, state-owned companies are able to sell their products at a low price because they don't properly cost their inputs. For example, a foreign barley malting company which provided malt to beer makers couldn't compete against its Chinese competitors who were selling malt at the cost of the barley without including the conversion costs.

In 1990 the central government announced that too many Western high-tech companies were off-loading old technology into China. They initiated the 'China Torch Program' to overcome this problem and create an indigenous high-technology capability. Between 1994 and 1998, 13 000 new Chinese companies in 52 high-tech parks generated over US$20 billion in sales revenue. Telephone switchboards, for example, had once been the preserve of overseas firms; now, Chinese competitors were producing world-class switchboards for a fraction of the cost of the imported models.

In 1864 the Hankow customs commissioner reported: 'Formidable opponents have arisen in the persons of Chinese, who forward foreign imports from Shanghai to Hankow, where, owing to their having no expensive establishments to maintain, they can undersell the foreign merchants.' (Hao 1970, p. 118)

A study of foreign companies in China from 1840 to 1937 concluded: ' . . . not all factors were in favour of foreign firms . . . Foreign firms not only had to pay a high salary to attract foreigners to work and stay in China but even had to pay a higher salary and wage scale to Chinese employees. The high scale could not be entirely justified on the grounds of high productivity.' (Hou 1965, p. 145)

But there are companies that have been profitable in the Chinese market despite competition from Chinese companies. Up until 1950 the British American Tobacco Company (BAT) made higher profits from its cigarettes in China than in the US, even though its cigarettes in China were 40 per cent cheaper (Cochran 1980, p. 73).

The company used aggressive competitive practices against the local Chinese competition. BAT distributors undercut local brands by lowering prices on equivalent cigarettes or by introducing new brands that directly challenged the local brand quality level. One tactic was for BAT agents to buy all the rival Chinese-owned Nanyang-brand cigarettes on the market, hold them until they became mouldy, and then dump them at low prices on traditional Nanyang customers. BAT did this in the middle of one of Nanyang's marketing campaigns. Outraged Nanyang customers had to be reimbursed and

Nanyang's reputation was seriously damaged, to the advantage of BAT (Cochran 1980, p. 62).

Unlike many Western companies, BAT did not confine itself to the major port cities. It advertised everywhere in the interior of China. When the owner of the Chinese Nanyang Cigarette Company travelled along the Yangtze valley to find out why his company's marketing efforts had been unsuccessful there, he found that wherever he went 'the streets and by-ways were covered with BAT advertisements, shopkeepers were committed to sell BAT cigarettes exclusively, and customers were loyal to BAT brands' (Cochran 1980, p. 72). In 1916 he toured to Kalgan, on the edge of the Mongolian steppes, just inside the Great Wall. He reported that there were 'no Western inns and even the Chinese inns are vile. Electric lights and jinrickshas have not been introduced. There is no way to get around except on horseback, in mule carts, and on foot. The wind fills the air with horse dung'. Even in this 'bitter, barren' place, he found two BAT representatives, both Westerners who were fluent in the local dialect, which he, a Cantonese, was not (Cochran 1980, p. 85).

When a marketing executive in a water heater manufacturing company was asked recently if the company had local competition, he replied without the slightest hesitation: 'You betcha!' Since the manufacturing joint venture began in 1996, over 100 Chinese companies have copied the water heater style and colouring. However, the local brands are poor in quality with just a two-year lifetime, compared with ten years for the joint venture company's heaters.

The executive's competitive strategy is based on brand strength. According to his reasoning, brand strength would attract a lot of people wanting to sell the product. Indeed, Chinese distribution companies wanted to call themselves 'Hotflow Nanjing' or 'Hotflow Shenyang', but this was resisted because distributors can fail to live up to their initial performance or go to a competitor, but still trade on the 'Hotflow' reputation.

By maintaining control of the brand and the name, the manufacturer can continue to have direct links with the market.

The joint venture company found that there were a lot of distributors who wanted exclusive rights for their area, but they turned out to be the type to collect exclusive agencies and then sit back and wait for the telephone to ring. Other distributors who have had some initial success may start to play the 'If . . . , then . . . ' game. They say things like, 'We've been talking to your competitor and they will give us better rebates and free advertising. They are also going to buy us a car. If you will . . . , then . . . '. The marketing executive has now adopted a scatter-gun approach to finding distributors. He appoints a number of distributors in each city on a trial basis. If they perform well and build the market, they sign distribution agreements; if their performance is lacking, they are culled. This gives the company maximum flexibility. Based on his early mistakes, his advice is not to set down procedures that have worked in the West, but to adapt to the local scene. He himself now uses the 'If . . . , then . . . ' strategy: 'If you sell X amount, then we will co-advertise in your area for Y dollars.' So far it has worked: his company is profitable, and they have retained control of their trademark.

Another approach to controlling competition is to have arrangements with the government in Beijing, although this won't necessarily guarantee protection from local competitors. Even the support of elder statesman Deng Xiaoping couldn't prevail against local government competition when Singaporean investors invested US$131 million in the Suzhou Industrial Park. The park was meant to show the Chinese best practice in the treatment of international investors. But a Suzhou vice mayor promoted a rival park with lower rentals and cheaper land which netted Motorola, Sony Chemicals and Philips Electronics. Meanwhile, Singapore's Suzhou Industrial Park was held up by delays in building its infrastructure. The Singaporeans mistakenly believed, as one businessman put it, 'that an agreement with the top would go all the way through the system like a lightning bolt'. He discovered that in China things don't work the Singapore way. Suzhou mayor, Chen Deming, advised his ethnic Chinese Singaporean brothers, 'When you or your joint venture partner decide to invest in China you must take into account our cultural preferences' (Dolven 1999).

Counterfeiting

One of the commonest forms of competition from Chinese companies is through counterfeiting foreign products. The Mars Confectionery company had just introduced their M&Ms (chocolate-coated candies) to the Chinese market when Chinese confectionery makers copied them and sold them as W&Ws. The W&Ws packet was identical to the Mars packet, except for the inversion of the name. Imported printing technology had no doubt made exact copying of the packaging very easy. The local product was put on the shelves next to the Mars product, but the price tag was half that of the American brand. Mars were worried that if people bought the inferior and cheaper local product, it would damage future sales of the genuine article, so it launched a court case. Within a year, W&Ws were removed from the city stores, but enforcement was slow and difficult in provincial towns in Zhejiang province where the local manufacturers had their factory.

The Coca-Cola company, whose product is copied all over China, sometimes uses less legal-based methods to control local entrepreneurs. On Hainan Island the Coca-Cola bottlers were given special incentives to report copies directly to the local city authorities, who dealt with the problem quickly. This has been an effective strategy.

International competition

Competition occurs not only between Chinese and foreign companies, but also between the many foreign companies in China who see China as the 'last great market'. The Chinese government has encouraged this thinking in a number of industrial sectors. A few foreign companies first set up operations; others who are concerned about being left out then petition the government. Although it appears difficult at first for them to enter the market, eventually the government eases the regulations. Foreign companies then flood in, creating a chronic excess capacity. This has happened in motorcycles, telecommunications, pharmaceuticals, beer and packaging.

There is US$140 billion of foreign investment in infrastructure. Foreign executives ask themselves: 'What do you do when there is overcapacity? You can't take your investment away again, you have to put product through it, so you have to lower your domestic prices to compete with everybody else.' Their complaint is that the Chinese community is getting access to state-of-the-art infrastructure at a return on capital that is disproportionately low, and that the foreign reserves are being built up because China has a whole wave of new capacity to service export markets at normal returns.

Foreign companies have complained to Beijing many times about excess approvals. They were reassured that approvals were being monitored and that there would be a limit to ensure that the growth of capacity was appropriate. This hasn't turned out to be the case. The effect of this competition is that, for many companies, prices are 20–30 per cent below what they budgeted. Only those Western companies which have been protected from competition by the Chinese government, such as Volkswagen in Shanghai, have been able to dominate their industry sector. Volkswagen has 60 per cent of the automobile market. However, it too may soon face the wild winds of competition as central protection and market control is withdrawn.

Despite foreign complaints about the lack of profitability due to overcapacity, Chinese policy-makers are worried about foreign domination of key industry sectors. They are concerned that Chinese national enterprises are in an unfavourable position because of the preferential treatment given to foreign-invested enterprises, and that pivotal industries such as automobiles and communications are monopolised by multinational companies, while chemicals and electronics are increasingly so (Tang 1995).

Smuggling

Smugglers are a third source of competition for foreign companies producing in China or exporting to China. The little old ladies who go across the Hong Kong/China border with a dozen hair shampoo bottles in a plastic carry bag are part of the smuggling system. Goods are smuggled in through Hong Kong by PRC trading firms who have the protection of regional governments and expertise in forging the documentation. They avoid the tariffs imposed on legally imported goods, which may be 40 per cent or higher. They are then easily able to undercut the legitimately imported product, as well as goods manufactured in China. These goods undersell the goods transported through legitimate channels and take away the livelihood of the legitimate distributors. Manufacturers in China end up competing against their own product.

Some foreign companies turn smuggling to their own advantage. For example, Chinese intermediaries may take the company's goods in through Guangdong and Fujian, where they have local contacts in the customs department and they pay a small import tariff. The goods are then transported north to provinces where the Chinese intermediaries have no contacts in the customs service. Were they to go straight to Tianjin or other northern ports, they would incur high duties.

3

Corruption: 'Legitimate loot'

Corruption in all its forms—fraud, smuggling, piracy, extortion, misuse of public funds, nepotism—is abundantly observable in contemporary China. Chinese television news regularly shows footage of illegal activities, particularly by the sons and daughters of officials. There are the famous cases, such as the suicide in 1995 of the vice mayor of Beijing, Wang Baosen, who was accused of extracting bribes for construction permits. His co-accused, the mayor of Beijing, Chen Xitong, was later dismissed from office.

Corruption in China is brought to the attention of foreign business people by its frequency and the involvement of officials. Corruption occurs in all societies, but its incidence and the form it takes differ according to the context. China is perceived by Western business people as the sixth most corrupt Asian country after Indonesia, Vietnam, India, Thailand and the Philippines. On the Corruption Perception Index where 10 indicates 'totally corruption-free', Indonesia scored 2, China 3.5, the United States 7.5, the United Kingdom and Australia 8.7, Canada 9.2 and Denmark 10 (Transparency International 1998).

There are a number of ways of understanding the prevalence of corruption and malfeasance in China. To

24

go to the deepest level of reasoning concerns the ethics of human relationships, beginning with the family.

Family obligations

In 1936, Lin Yutang wrote *My Country and My People* to interpret China to the West. He explained corruption and nepotism as 'necessary' because of the Chinese family system. Here I will use his explanation of his own people. Confucianism placed the family as the foundation of the social system. Social obligations were all contained by the 'five cardinal relationships': ruler–subject, father–son, husband–wife, older brother–younger brother, and friend–friend. Three of the five obligations are about relations between family members, and friend–friend can be identified with the family because friends can be included in the family circle.

In formulating the social order, Confucius omitted a man's relationship with strangers. This led to what Lin calls 'a lack of the social mind': 'The family, with its friends, became a walled castle, with the greatest communistic co-operation and mutual help within . . . outside which everything is legitimate loot.' (Lin 1939, p. 172)

The 'evils of the family system' were documented early in China's history by Hanfeizi (d. 233 BC), a politician and philosopher who served the First Emperor of China until he was forced by a rival to commit suicide: 'The breaking down of the civil service system through nepotism and favouritism, robbing the nation to enrich the family, the erection of rich villas by politicians, the absence of any punishment for offending officials, the consequent absence of "public citizenship" and general lack of social consciousness.' (Lin 1939, p. 170)

Many foreign business people would see parallels with contemporary China in Hanfeizi's description. Hanfeizi advocated law as the fundamental means of government to rectify these problems—an approach that was not adopted by following dynasties.

Lin Yutang's conclusion is that the strongest ethic among the majority of Chinese is the benefit to family and friends: 'The minister who robs the nation to feed the family, either for the present or for the next three or four generations, by amassing half a million to ten million dollars, is only trying to glorify his ancestors and be a "good" man of the family. Graft, or "squeeze" may be a public vice, but is always a family virtue.'

A young Chinese professional, when asked how he saw his responsibilities in life, said: 'Be a good man first, behave in a way to succeed in society, educate your children, look after your wife, maintain a harmonious family life, ensure that your family is good within society. Then if you can do that you can do something more. You can go out into society, you can do something for the government, you could be an official. After that you will have an important position and you can use your knowledge to influence people around you and achieve a better place for all people.' (Atkinson 1998)

Although this young man was educated through the communist system, his values are remarkably similar to Lin Yutang's traditional Chinese family values.

Another outcome of the duties to family and friends is nepotism. Lin says: 'A successful man, if he is an official, always gives the best jobs to his relatives, and if there are not ready jobs he can create sinecure ones . . . A minister does not place only his nephews in the ministry, but he also has to place the nephews of other high officials . . . who write him letters of recommendation. Where is he going to place them, except in sinecure posts and "advisorships"? The economic pressure and the pressure of overpopulation are so keen . . . that every new organ or every official assuming a new post is daily flooded with, literally, hundreds of letters of recommendation.' (Lin 1939, pp. 172–3)

It is not surprising that Western managers find their Chinese staff recommending relatives for positions in the company, or their Chinese managers appointing relatives of officials to positions for which they are not qualified.

The Chinese are simply following the dictum, 'charity begins at home'.

Lin Yutang makes one other observation about why family has such power over individuals. He believes that the family system 'very nearly takes the place of religion by giving man a sense of immortality, and through the ancestral worship it makes the sense of immortality very vivid' (Lin 1939, p. 168). Modern city families do not practise ancestral worship, but train children to feel 'obligation and gratitude to their parents, and respect for elders', thus coming close to Lin's belief that family continuity has a religious-like function in Chinese society.

The idea of 'family as the basis of morality' was brought home to me when a Chinese family was visiting my property in the Australian countryside. The young son caught some tadpoles from the lake and was going to take them home in a jar. His mother said to him, 'You cannot do that. Put them back. They have family.' He saw his mistake and returned the tadpoles to the lake.

Sharing: *'Zhanguang'* and reciprocity

It was customary in China in the old days for a wealthy or influential man with no sons, to support a poor but talented youth, by providing for his education and organising his early career. The patron expects that in return, when the youth is in a position of power and influence, he will favour members of the patron's family.

This happened in the case of Chiang Kai-shek, the Guomindang leader of the 1930s and 1940s who ultimately sought refuge in Taiwan before the victorious communist forces assumed control of China in 1949. His patron's name was Chen Chimei. He sent Chiang to the military academy at Baodingfu and to Japan to study military organisation and tactics. Later Chiang repaid his debt by promoting his patron's sons Chen Guofu and Chen Lifu to head one of his secret intelligence services.

They were referred to as the C.C. Clique (Lattimore 1990, pp. 146–7).

While patronage has an element of 'nepotism' deriving from the family system, it has another value underlying it. This is 'sharing', or *zhanguang*—the characters literally mean 'sharing in the light' (Yan 1996, p. 128). A person 'standing in the light', which means he has abundant privileges and contacts, as well as material goods, is expected to share them with others connected to him. The Chinese have a saying which describes how such a person shares benefits with his associates: '*Yiren de dao, jiquan sheng tian*': ('When a man attains the Tao, his chickens and dogs ascend with him to heaven').

This is different from the Christian view which centres on individual redemption and faith: 'No man cometh unto the Father, but by me' (John 14:6); 'Work out your own salvation with fear and trembling' (Philippians 2:12); and 'Oh put not your trust in princes, nor in any child of man: for there is no help in them (*Prayer Book 1662*, 146:2). For the Chinese, an individual is defined by relationships with and responsibilities to his family and friends.

A foreign businessman received a graphic lesson in the ethics of family and *zhanguang* from his Chinese business associates. He was hosting a visit of five Chinese businessmen to discuss their joint project. Waiting at the airport to welcome them, he was astounded when the five approached him accompanied by another 32 people. When the businessman asked his Chinese associates about the crowd, he was told by the leader, 'These are my family and friends. They have come for a sightseeing holiday. I am responsible for them. Where I go, my family will follow.' The foreigner, having taken the lesson, went off to hire a bus (Atkinson 1998).

Just how deeply held these values of sharing and reciprocity are is demonstrated in the emotional response of many Chinese when these values are transgressed or ignored. When two Australian professors went to China as part of an institutional 'friendly relationship', they were shown great hospitality. But the thing which brought down opprobrium on their heads from the Chinese side was their failure, when out visiting local tourist sights, to 'spontaneously' buy cans of soft drink for their Chinese hosts. Instead, they said they were thirsty and thus put the hosts in the situation of having to buy drinks for them. The Australians were quite oblivious of the requirement that the most affluent must show generosity by 'sharing', and of the effect this had on the Chinese. The Chinese discussed this among themselves. They dubbed the two visitors, 'Professor Greedy' and 'Professor Mean'. To the Chinese the professors came from a wealthy country and obviously had private means. They should therefore have understood the ethics of *zhanguang*. The Australian point of view was that their stay in China was financially supported by the Chinese side, as part of the friendly relationship agreement, and they just assumed that the Chinese would look after all aspects of their stay in China.

When the next group from the same institution went to China, the Chinese working in Australia advised their colleagues in China not to put themselves out of pocket on the Australians' behalf by inviting them to their homes, buying gifts and escorting them everywhere, because the Australians had no appreciation of the duties of sharing and reciprocity that this required. Of course, the Chinese had expected that they would receive on-going benefits from the Australians in return for their hospitality. What they had come up against was a different value system where the more affluent is not morally obliged to the less affluent, where favours are not necessarily dispensed in return for favours, and where being 'friends' does not translate into giving commercial preference.

Confucius said, 'A man of humanity, wishing to establish his own character, also establishes the character of others, and wishing to be prominent himself, also helps others to be prominent'. (Chan 1969, p. 31, 6:28) This is known as the 'golden rule', a thread running through the Confucian texts. The whole gift-giving culture is premised on the value of reciprocity. You give the gift first, hoping to induce reciprocity later. In the West, gift-giving usually takes place after an interaction, as an expression of gratitude.

The squeeze

A famous Chinese scholar of the 1930s, Gu Hongming, said that the commonest conjugation in Chinese grammar is that of the verb 'to squeeze' (Lin 1939, p. 173). It conjugates regularly: 'I squeeze, you squeeze, he squeezes; we squeeze, you squeeze, they squeeze.' The *Oxford Dictionary* definition is 'a forced exaction or impost made by Asiatic officials or servants; a percentage taken on goods bought or sold; an illegal charge or levy'. The date this usage came into the English language was 1858, as Englishmen extended their trading in China following the Opium Wars.

The squeeze was well known among foreigners in China up until 1949. It was levied by everyone from mandarins to 'house boys'. An Englishman resident in Shanghai described his experience of the squeeze. An English friend had recommended a Chinese carpenter who did a very good job of building some bookshelves. Some time later he asked Chang, his butler, to send for him again to do some more carpentry work. When someone else arrived to do the work, he asked Chang what had happened. 'Chang replied, "That other carpenter very bad man". "He wasn't," I said, "he did very good work." "This carpenter much more better," Chang said, and that was the end of it.' Apparently the first carpenter had cheated Chang out of his expected commission (Ward 1969).

Another story from the same period is from a New Zealander travelling up the Yangtze River and staying in

Chinese inns, not noted during those times for their cleanliness or hospitality.

'The hotel cook informed me that, according to the custom prevailing in all first-class hotels, he had prepared a dinner for me at his own expense, simply, as he said, that the distinguished foreigner might speak well of him in distant countries; but in reality to "squeeze" the stranger . . . The dinner was very good; but I had to pay very dearly for it. Before we left I handed him five taels, enough to pay for his dinner three times over, and leave a very handsome tip; but the rascal pocketed the money, and very coolly asked me for another three taels for the dinner presented by him. It was no use growling. "Custom", universal tyrant, was appealed to, and I was obliged to pay.' (Cooper 1871, p. 161)

A modern version of the common 'squeeze' is the following observed by a Western businessman: 'Everyone builds in a personal payment factor. The general manager of a state enterprise may not be able to touch the finances of the factory, but he can make money by putting a margin on every sale or purchase. Part of the margin goes back to his bosses on the board of directors or at the county office. These are personal payments. Unless this happens he will lose his position. There is a constant rising and falling of people.'

Bureaucratic corruption

Corruption in the bureaucracy is aided, and in fact made inevitable, by the principle of 'entrusted' or 'inherent power' within the legal and administrative system. 'Inherent power' gives bureaucrats discretion in the interpretation of central laws and regulations, the implementation of laws and regulations, and law-making within their own jurisdiction. The two controlling elements on the power of officials are Party discipline, which in very serious cases is harsh, and personal morality. In a recent case the former vice-governor of Hubei province was expelled from the Communist Party for corruption. The judgment of the Communist Party of China Central Commission for Discipline Inspection stated that 'he never attached importance to study and self-improvement . . . and cherished no ideals for lofty pursuits' (*Beijing Review* 1999). Thus, personal morality was seen as the controlling mechanism of official corruption, and it had failed him.

Responsiveness to the best interests of one's locality is one of the underlying rationales for the discretion given to bureaucrats. China is seen as too big and diverse for centrally proclaimed laws and regulations to be appropriate in detail for every locale. Thus, laws are written in the general and applied in the particular by local officials.

The practical operations of this system are described below from a Chinese perspective. This account is based on advice offered by a Chinese researcher from Sichuan, Zhu Xinmin, to Western business people. He describes how to approach bureaucrats to ask them to make an exception to the regulations in your favour.

First, the officials need to consider:

- who issued the regulations; and
- what impact an exception will have on public opinion.

If their own office issued the regulations and they assess the consequences of making an exception as positive, it will not be a problem to make your case an exception to the published regulations.

If the regulations were issued by another administration, and the officials assess the outcome as positive, they will:

- refer you to a contact in the other administration; or
- help you to organise your case; or
- help by acting as go-betweens.

Zhu comments: 'Of course, this calls for a close friendship.'

If the regulations were issued by their superior administration and the officials consider the outcomes to be positive to local interests, with no negative outcomes for others, the industry public administrator will need to accompany you to meet the local leader in charge of the matter.

If you can convince the local leader of your case, he will direct the administrator to prepare a report to the superior administration petitioning for an exception to the regulations. This will take a minimum of a month. Again, a curious comment by Zhu: 'Of course, this calls for an even further closer friendship than the case before.'

This is the process from a Chinese perspective of how officials are able to exercise their inherent power and interpret or change regulations, but 'close friendship' and 'even further closer friendship' are essentials in achieving your aims.

Zhu draws the line between this process and that of corruption: 'What is regarded as malpractice and corruption is both breach of a regulation issued by the superior administration without permission and intention for either a private or collective gain of the official concerned.' (Zhu 1996, p. 277)

A positive outcome was achieved through official discretion by a Western businessman who had a legal problem of titles to land and equipment in a joint venture. The joint venture agreement, which had been signed, specified that the Chinese partner's titles were clear. The partner was a government department. However, it turned out that they had none of the titles. Both the land and the equipment were mortgaged to Chinese banks. The foreign manager told the vice mayor that unless something was done to establish clear title the joint venture would collapse, as title was required to borrow working capital. The vice mayor said simply, 'In China we have rule by man. Man makes the law.' His unspoken implication was: 'Man can *change* the law.' He told the Western businessman, 'Don't worry about it. Get on with your business. The problem will be solved.' He and his senior bureaucrats set a process in motion through the bureaucracy and six months later both titles were cleared.

Officials have discretionary power over the allocation of resources and land, over the issuing of permits for construction, power, water and other facilities. They collect taxes for both the locality and the central government. In the twenty or so years since China's economy has opened to the West, demand has exceeded supply in many areas, from consumer products, to construction materials, transport and land. Officials who have power over these areas use this opportunity to derive benefits for themselves, their families and friends, and for their work organisations. It isn't difficult for them to undertake extortion through imposing fees for what should be normally provided services.

There are not the institutional checks and balances on official power that exist in most Western economies. Officials have always had a large number of prerogatives. One was to use public funds under their trust for their own personal ends, as long as the money was eventually repaid. This tradition, called *nuo yong*, or 'to shift and use', was originally instituted because the living expenses and government operating budgets came from local collections. In 1988, this 'loan' period was specified as three months.

When the benefits are directed to the work group or organisation, such as the military, it is common for a culture of silence to develop around it, for two reasons. One is that the benefits are shared. The second is that officials are accountable only to their superiors who are outside the work group. Within their own work groups they have power over rewards and punishments of subordinates; they are both judge and policeman.

In government law-making on corruption, two definitions are employed: 'using one's authority for private ends' and 'using public resources to manufacture private ones'. The 1988 Provisional Regulations on the Penalties for Corruption and Bribery of State Administrative Personnel specified accepting gifts, commissions and administrative fees, and soliciting forms of income not specified by the state as corrupt practices. 'Bureaucratism', or 'acting like a bureaucrat' was also condemned in the administrative regulations. It was defined as squandering public money, enjoying special privileges, using the back door—or *guanxi* (that is, obtaining limited resources through personal contacts rather than using legitimate channels) and cliquism. One of the commonest abuses has always been *da chi, da he*, or 'big eating, big drinking'. Various forms of self-aggrandisement happen in China, as they happen all over the world (Kwong 1997).

The following passage, adapted from Liu Zhenyun (1994), gives an insight into the social pressures that facilitate corruption among officials, despite the existence of disciplinary procedures aimed at eradicating it. Deputy Prefect Jin is sent to investigate four former colleagues accused of diverting public funds to build themselves elaborate houses. He started with Cong, with whom he had worked during the 'Four Cleanups' movement. When he arrived at Cong's office, he asked: 'Where's Cong?' The manager stammered: 'I think he's in a meeting, sir. Shall I go and find him for you?' Jin pursued the matter: 'What meeting? Where's the meeting being held? At what level, district or provincial? I don't suppose the central leadership sent a special plane for him. Tell me straight, where did he go?'

The manager, looking extremely embarrassed, blurted out: 'Secretary Cong is building a house in the north of the county. He hasn't shown up for work for two days. I'll send someone to fetch him right away.' But Jin stopped him. 'There's no need for that. I'll go and find him myself.' He jumped back into his car and told the driver, 'Take me to the Beiguan area'.

On arriving at their destination, Jin found that Cong was indeed building a house. So, the report was correct! He had even requisitioned a crane. It was going to be a two-storey building, and the first storey was just about finished. It was in the style of a palace, clad in creamy-white tiles that dazzled the eye. It took up a large area.

When Jin's car drew up to the building site, Cong was already there to greet his visitor, a big grin on his face. It was obvious that he had been expecting Jin. The latter got out of his car and asked, 'How did you know I was coming?'

Cong replied, 'I guessed'. Then he went on matter-of-factly: 'The office manager telephoned.' They lit cigarettes. Then Cong noticed the entourage following Jin. 'What have you come for,' he asked, 'with that crowd in your wake?'

It was Jin's turn to be matter-of-fact. 'To investigate you,' he said. 'To find out who is building this house.'

'Well, investigate,' Cong said with a laugh, putting his wrists together as if inviting Jin to handcuff him. Jin joined in his merriment.

Cong got into Jin's car with him, and the two cars sped off towards the local guesthouse. On their way, Cong said, 'I've got a sheep from Inner Mongolia. How about making it into a hotpot?'

'There's no need for that,' retorted Jin. 'Just get someone to get hold of some live fish that I can take back in the car with me for my superior, Mr Wu, the prefect.'

At lunchtime Jin and Cong dined together, while the manager hosted the rest of the work team in a separate room. They ate mutton hotpot. After a few mouthfuls, Jin said, 'Cong, my dear fellow, we have always got along well together, so let me be frank with you. We have had many years of Party training and we are old cadres. I don't understand how you, Zhou, Hu and Bai can suddenly start building your own private houses.'

Cong took a shot of liquor before answering, 'We're well into our fifties. About to retire. We're not like you, climbing the ladder of promotion. Oh, no. What chance of promotion have we got now? Retirement. Retirement's looming. And when one is to retreat from the frontline, one needs a road to retreat down. After working without a break for the Party all these years, don't you think we deserve safe havens to retire to? People have feelings, you know. When I retire, do you want me to go and live in a slum? Now here you are feasting on old Cong's mutton hotpot, aren't you?'

Jin took another cigarette. He looked at Cong but didn't say a word. The two of them carried on with their hotpot. Finally Jin said, 'Well, of course it's alright to build a house. There's nothing wrong with that. If ordinary people are allowed to build houses, then county Party secretaries should be allowed to, too. It's just that this is an awkward time for you to be building a house; it's running head-on against Party policy.'

Cong said, 'I don't give a damn about whether it conflicts with Party policy or not. I'm paying for it myself—the bricks, timber, cement, sand, the land—it's all coming out of my pocket.'

Jin said, 'Well, of course I have to make an investigation into these things. You bought the land and the building materials yourself. That's right. It's just that, er, where did the money come from? I mean, most other people wouldn't be able to afford it. How big is that courtyard, for instance? It's huge, isn't it? Well, if that isn't a reckless encroachment on arable land, I don't know what is!'

Cong was indignant, 'I'm encroaching on arable land? Well, what about your district administration? I suppose all the work's done while you're hovering in the air! What about District Party Secretary Lu's house—and Prefect Wu's? They're no smaller than mine. I think you should go and investigate up there. You'll really find something worth investigating. You should be on the Party Discipline Inspection Committee; your talents are wasted down here!'

After lunch they went into a room in the guesthouse where they each lay down on a bed. Their conversation turned to family matters. Jin took out a massage device and gave it to Cong for his wife to use on her bad back. They chatted until after two o'clock, when Cong said: 'Never mind, you just go back. I'll have the County Discipline Inspection Committee write a report, with a list of the land and materials expenses appended to it.

That way you'll be off the hook.' Jin nodded, and then asked, 'What about Zhou, Hu and Bai? Do I have to go chasing after them?'

Cong thought deeply for a minute, and then said: 'It would be better if you didn't. You and I are very close, so it doesn't matter if you chase me. But I'm not so sure about the others. The thing is, you can't afford to lose the support of several counties. How could you do a proper job as deputy prefect? I'll have a word to them and get them to clean up their acts.'

As they left the room together, Cong said: 'I made a trip to Chungong county a few days ago.'

'Did you meet any of my family?' Jin asked.

'Of course,' Cong replied. 'And I can report that your younger sister and brother are fine. And your nephews are doing very well. They all send their regards and say you are very selfish.'

'Selfish? Me? Don't take any notice of that nonsense.' Jin was amused.

'They say all you care about is your job; you don't give a thought to them at all. If it's not too difficult,' Cong ventured, 'you could try to move them up to the district where you are, couldn't you?'

'Oh, they'll have to be patient,' Jin said. 'It's only a matter of time, after all.'

Cong nodded in agreement.

'Well, look after yourself,' Jin said, climbing into his car.

'Goodbye,' said Cong. The car swept out of the county town, with Jin Quanli sprawled in the back.

Two weeks later Jin received reports from the Party committees of Zhou, Cong, Hu and Bai's counties. He passed them on to District Party Secretary Lu for his approval. Lu said, 'Since the investigations turned up nothing of any great importance, I think we can consider the matter closed.'

It is obvious from this account that officials are in tight networks where reciprocity is expected, and where there is pressure to observe the values of face and goodwill towards friends. Cong played cleverly on Jin's status as deputy prefect, urging him to 'share the light' with subordinates and family. He also used the technique of pointing to what his superiors were doing in building large houses and administration buildings. The Chinese have a saying: *'Shang xing, xia xiao'*—'What the superior does, those below copy.'

Participation in corruption is a dangerous road for foreign companies, however, and most try to abide by their rules of corporate governance.

4

Communication

Some of the ways in which the Chinese communicate are
fundamentally different from those of Westerners. It is
commonly stated that the Chinese see information as
power, and restrict it at all levels. For example, the
authorities keep information on regulations they have
promulgated within the bureaucracy for their discretionary application. Work groups trained by foreigners refuse
to train the next work group, because that might give
them an advantage. Chinese trainers may omit to impart
crucial information to trainees, in order to shore up their
own power. These are indicators of a society with a strong
hierarchical power structure. A person who can control
the flow of information is in a position to reinforce and
express his power over others.

Indirectness is another feature that distinguishes Chinese communication from Western communication. A
large concreting company had 100 concrete trucks sitting
on the wharf for weeks because one of the foreign staff
had upset the customs officers involved in clearing them
off the wharf. He had criticised them for being 'too slow'.
He then discovered what 'too slow' really was. Another
company had the power and water supplies to their
factory cut off without explanation. It turned out that
one of the company's Western managers was having a
relationship with a Chinese woman. The local authorities

were upset by this and signalled their disapproval by this indirect method.

Underlying differences

An early researcher into cultural differences, Edward T. Hall, divided cultures into two types according to the way they communicated. He called these two types 'high context' and 'low context'. Context refers to how one links to what is before, behind and around one, like words in a sentence. Hall defined these two types as follows:

1. *'High context' type (high degree of linkage to the context)*
   This person will talk round and round the point, expecting the other person to know what is bothering him. He puts all the pieces into place except the crucial one. That is the role of the other person. By talking round and round, the person tries to include the possible points of view of others to minimise disagreement. Third parties are used in sensitive situations and to resolve conflict situations.
2. *'Low context' type (low linkage to the context)*
   This person gets straight to the point. He emphasises overall structure, patterns and limits. He emphasises the task, rather than the relationships and people's feelings. 'Low context' people distrust the use of third parties.

China falls into the 'high context' type of culture, while most English-speaking cultures fall into the 'low context' type.

A similar conclusion was drawn by Linda Young (1994), who recorded business conversations at meetings involving Chinese and American managers. She also found that Chinese and American managers present their arguments differently. The Chinese first detail all the surrounding factors that might appeal to the listeners' motivations before putting forward their personal recommendations;

thus, they follow the 'high context' communication rules. Most Westerners put their recommendations first, and follow them with the reasons, because the task is more important than the relationships. A Chinese might sum up the American way of communicating as 'backwards, always giving their conclusion first' (Young 1994, p. 131).

The Chinese approach of including the group is embedded in the structure of the Chinese language. A Chinese sentence which is putting forward a point of view or recommendation must follow the sequence of: 'Because . . . , therefore . . . '

'Because . . . ' introduces the history, the background to the problem, and the chain of reasoning. 'Therefore . . . ' introduces the speaker's recommendation. The recommendation must come at the end of the sentence. The fact that this order is embedded in the grammatical structure of the sentence demonstrates how deep this sequence of thinking is. For English speakers it is more common to say, 'I believe . . . because . . . ', or 'I recommend such-and-such because . . . '.

So, the Chinese 'high context' type of communication results in a sequence of communication that aims to minimise disagreements by including the possible points of view of others before the individual's point is put forward—if it is at all. It may well be omitted. A Chinese person's favoured sequence in expressing a point of view is usually as follows:

1. *Favourable statements, generalised praise such as difficulties overcome, contributions made, sacrifices and successes*
   In this part of the communication, the beginning, Westerners are trained to listen for the 'executive summary of recommendations'. When they don't get it, they get frustrated and dismiss what the Chinese person is telling them as irrelevant or illogical. It could also be interpreted as evasive, 'beating around the bush' or as having something to hide.
2. *Unfavourable statements and statements of discontent*
   Problems are raised as recommendations. There is an

emphasis on mutual benefit, the common good, respect. But an individual's name or specific circumstances are not given.

While the Chinese are following the 'Because . . . , therefore . . . ' sequence, most Westerners won't be paying attention because under Western rules of communication this part of the message is subordinate to the first part. Because they have 'switched off' here, they won't hear the really important points a Chinese person is making indirectly, relying on the listener to put it all together. As a result, they are in danger of concluding that everything is okay (Brick 1991).

For the Chinese, to follow the Western order in putting their point of view would be to risk appearing rude, because it would sound as if they were demanding something. They would fear losing face as a result of acting selfishly and aggressively without consideration for others in the group.

The members of a Chinese work group consider it a smart strategy not to start with a request which may not be granted by the chairman and would lead to loss of respect from others in the team. Acting in a Western way would also be dangerous because the speaker wouldn't know what the others were planning to ask. Whereas Americans are trained in public speaking skills, the stress in Chinese upbringing at home and at school is on listening skills.

In my experience, many Westerners don't listen intently or with enough patience to Chinese speakers, and consequently they don't hear the actual point of view of the speaker. Quite often they will cut the Chinese speaker off before he reaches his main point. They have already dismissed the initial 'context' setting as rambling, disconnected and not 'to the point'.

This Chinese form of communication is intimately connected to protecting 'face', as illustrated in the following interchange. A foreign general manager wanted to speak to the Chinese chairman of the Chinese partner about some supply problems they were experiencing. The manager's Chinese assistant advised him: 'Tell them that through all the efforts up until now co-operation with this supplier has progressed pretty smoothly.' The foreign general manager replied, 'But that's not true.' The Chinese assistant said, 'If you mention to the chairman that you are not happy with the supplier, he will treat it as a loss of face before his counterparts on the Australian board. That would make things even worse' (Orton 1997).

In addition to 'high context' and 'face' influences on Chinese communication practices, there is also the influence of status. The way a Chinese subordinate communicates with the boss differs from comparable communication in a Western workplace. Chinese subordinates want to be 'non-face-threatening' towards the boss. They are modest in referring to themselves and reluctant to impose their point of view. They are opening the way for the superior to impose his or her own judgment and intention (Young 1994). One writer who investigated boss–subordinate behaviour in Chinese organisations in Taiwan said: 'To publicly express alternative ideas is to express lack of confidence in the boss. Such expressions are ultimately threatening to his position as chief, and, at least vaguely, disrespectful.' (Silin 1976, p. 65)

These attitudes and beliefs of Chinese employees are misconstrued by many Westerners, who describe Chinese employees as 'unable to take authority', 'unable to be self-managing' and 'timid'.

Another useful classification of Western–Chinese communication is 'conceptual communication'—that is, the notion that words don't necessarily conjure up the same concept in another culture. For example, the word 'quality' will mean something quite different to someone who has experienced the best the world has to offer, compared to the mental picture it conjures up for someone whose lifestyle is far more modest. Because Chinese and Westerners have such different background experiences, many expatriate managers come to learn that practical demonstration of an idea is more useful than a generalised directive.

Trainers from Giordano, the highly successful Hong Kong retail merchandiser whose credo is 'Giordano means service', were attempting to train Guangzhou shop assistants to smile, bow and greet customers with the phrase 'Welcome to Giordano'. The Chinese girls refused, saying: 'That is like prostitutes selling their smiles.' Here the 'conceptual' communication produced very different images in the minds of the Chinese shop assistants from those intended by the Hong Kong trainers. The deadlock was resolved by all the senior managers taking their turn to greet customers outside the shop. The Chinese shop assistants got the 'conceptual' message, saw the delight on customers' faces and adopted the procedure.

Strategies

Western managers can learn a new way of approaching communication with the Chinese. Here are two insightful examples, the first from a private businessman and the second from the technical director of Shanghai Volkswagen.

'We have had problems measuring the land in southern China. We work around it indirectly. We say, "Do you really think this land is as big as what it says on the plan? Let's walk around and measure it". So we walk, say, 1600 metres around the whole fence measuring it. After adding the whole thing up, it comes to 59.5 hectares rather than the 60 hectares it says on the plan. We say, "We'd better change that on the plan". If you confront it directly and criticise the plan, you might as well forget about it. Everyone will walk away in a huff.'

Here the manager has adopted an indirect method of dealing with a problem that could easily cause a loss of face by the Chinese side.

And now the technical director from Shanghai

Volkswagen: ' . . . the real problem [rather than the technical problem] was communication with the Chinese. In the beginning we were rather bad at listening to what the Chinese were saying, as opposed to hearing what we thought they should be saying. Gradually, I came to learn something about their expectations. They expect top management to go out and talk to them, asking them about their problems . . . If you do not engage directly in all these processes you will fail. You have to get the necessary feedback, and going down to talk to them is the only way.' (Hoon-Halbauer 1996, p. 205)

This manager had to overcome two common obstacles to Western–Chinese communication: his own perceptions of the Chinese as equal partners, and the Western impatience with the Chinese communication style. Here he has learned to listen, and to wait for Chinese opinion to emerge from the discussion.

The American company Russell & Co. successfully ran steamships on the Yangtze River during the latter half of the nineteenth century. Because they targeted the Chinese rather than the foreign communities of Shanghai as customers for travel and shipment of goods, their relations with the Chinese were of critical importance. R.B. Forbes, the managing director, selected American clerks in part for their ability to 'talk to the Chinese'. Writing to a sponsor of a new clerk from New York, he said: 'He will be brought at once into contact with the Chinese, and will learn how to deal with them . . . an important point in a clerk's training out here.' One of the characteristics he praised was a clerk's ability to be 'pliant with the Chinese' (Liu 1962, pp. 91–92). It is apparent that the art of communicating with the Chinese is deserving of attention.

The situation most liable to cause culture shock in Westerners is negotiating with the Chinese. Their preference for indirect communication confuses Westerners. A Western businessman with long experience of negotiating paper imports to China, technology transfer and manufacturing facilities described his perception and strategies as follows.

'If they want to buy X, they start trying to bargain for something lesser—Y. But after a little while they start edging back to talk about X. I never let them do that. I always say it's irrelevant because they are trying to buy Y. So I move them back all the time and keep taking them away from their end point.

'They are probably thinking, "We'll confuse these silly Westerners by starting to say we want to buy that, when in actual fact we want to buy this".

'Once I realise what they are really after, I never go to that. I push them away from what they want to do, and it becomes more and more obvious what they are after, and how keen they are to get that. I also start to get an inkling of why they want it. They keep trying to take the negotiations around to that item all the time. You've got to really know what they want, why they want it, and how strongly they want it.

'It takes a few meetings to understand which direction they are coming from.'

The Chinese here are using the common Sunzi *Art of War* strategy, 'Pretend to advance along one path while secretly going along another.'

The indirectness—or in Western terms, the failure to be open and state what the situation is—shows up when an agreement comes to the implementation stage. It is not uncommon for the Chinese to agree to a proposal but then to do nothing. The Westerner with whom they have made the agreement is expecting the action to follow, and is puzzled or angry when it does not. A manager trying to gain supplies said, 'Most often, they will smile and nod. Then nothing will happen' (Upton and Seet 1994).

The Chinese strategy of agreeing but taking no action allows them to withdraw without confrontation. Having been brought up in a 'high context' culture, they expect that the other party will read the hidden signals and deduce the actual situation. Unfortunately, people from a 'low context' culture such as the United States, Canada, Australia, Britain or New Zealand are not trained to read the signals. In deciding on their strategy, the Chinese focus on the practical difficulties entailed in putting the agreement into action, and the Westerners will generally be focusing on the legal responsibility to implement the agreement (Brick 1991).

There is another influence on Chinese negotiation style that disorients Westerners. This is the concept of the 'ingroup'. If the Chinese see their interlocutor as a member of the ingroup, they use the techniques of respect, mutual benefit and an emphasis on harmony. If the interlocutor is perceived as an outsider, however, the Chinese communication style will be dispassionate and rationalistic, without any regard for the outsider's feelings or needs. Their communication style can become anything but respectful and harmony-seeking. It will be abrupt, accusing and forceful, and could include shouting (Yates and Lee 1996). Many Western managers have experienced this style of communication, much to their amazement.

'In the negotiations the Chinese were incredibly rude to our face, saying: "What are you doing here? You don't even speak Chinese. What do you know about this? You aren't a Chinese lawyer." They were blunt, head-on.'

This aggressive style highlighted an attitude that appeared most inconsiderate to the European team. 'They insisted on starting the negotiations on a Monday morning. So our senior technical people flew over from the Netherlands. At nine o'clock on the Monday morning they said, "We're not ready for you. We'll do it next week, or the week after that". So our technical people had to either fly home or hang around in Beijing.'

This is a good example of different communication styles: the abrupt, rationalistic style of the Chinese dealing with outsiders when a European would expect politeness and apology. Because the style is not considered acceptable in a Western context, it can invite a negative and emotional response from a Westerner. Such a response then leads to negative feelings on the Chinese side. The most useful strategy is to realise this is a cross-cultural situation where the behaviour has different meanings. It is then easier to distance oneself emotionally and handle the communication effectively. It doesn't mean that you turn the other cheek, but that you harness your natural response and think rationally about your response strategy.

Case study: 'Often it is complicated'

A Western manager in Shanghai who speaks Chinese and whose wife is Chinese has adopted the following rules when communicating with his staff.

Harness your natural responses

Try not to get upset. Sometimes you think, 'This isn't going the right way'. So you try the foreigner's approach, saying: 'But it should be like this. This is how it's supposed to be done.' Ten years ago if you had said that they would have replied: 'No, no, no. This is China. You will do it the Chinese way.'

People don't do that so much these days. They hear you out and say: 'Yes, but . . . ' and they give you the reasons, so you can understand what brings about the events and why you have to go that way. Whereas before it was a complete rejection of your ideas, 'No, no, no. We don't do things that way. You have to learn how *we* do business.'

Try to listen and understand

Be patient. And if you can't understand, ask them to write it down and take it away and think about it for a while. Because often it is complicated. A lot of things are complicated in Shanghai. One of the big lessons is that nothing is as it seems on the surface. There are always intricate reasons and underlying reasons why someone is doing something. In business it is the same. You might have a government official who is confronting you about something. The reason is that behind him there is a competitor who is encouraging him to do that. Then it is hard to understand. That is when you have to sit down and listen and try and work out what the real game plan is. Then you have to bring in your own people to counter the attack. So it is best not to say, 'This is wrong. Do this', which is always a temptation. Most things I delay. If I can't understand it immediately, I just say: 'OK.' I write it down and then think about what to do next.

Try to be flexible

Don't ever draw a line and say, 'That's it. I won't go any further.' If you say that, they'll say: 'Well, it must be like this. I want it like this.' Always tell them, 'If you've got a different idea, I'd be interested to hear it.' If they have a different idea, you say: 'OK, I'll think about it.' You can't always make the right decision. Always revisit it.

Be fair in dealing with people

Anyone can walk in the door and tell me their problem. He has something he is upset about, so he wants to have his say. With 600 people that's sometimes a lot of time, but it's the only way to understand what's going on. Treat them fairly and with respect. You say to yourself, 'Is this thing an issue, or a non-issue?' And you try to find the truth. In Shanghai there are a lot of things underneath which are difficult for a foreigner *ever* to understand. You've got the feeling there is something underneath, but what is it? The Chinese have difficulty dealing with each other. My wife is Chinese. She says, 'I don't want to be with Chinese people. They are too complicated. I want to be in Australia where they are simple people.'

There's no doubt that some Australians are tricky. But for the Shanghainese it's a pastime. There is a word for it: *tiao jiangguo*, meaning 'to mix the gluepot so that you cannot see the truth'. You are trying to see what is underneath, but they're doing something up here, so you're looking up here, but the real thing is happening under there. That expression is very popular.

If you have loyalty and good systems, you can see through the *tiao jiangguo*. With foreign companies a lot of it is *tiao jiangguo*. They are more simple; they don't see things.

Keep an open mind, don't believe everything you are told, and find people you can trust who can tell you what is going on. So, here we foreigners are sitting at the top. Underneath there are 595 other people, all into *tiao jiangguo*. You put in a management team who are loyal and who you can trust. That group underneath the foreigners, although there are Chinese in the top group too, is very important. You have to get young people who have some ambition, who have some loyalty to individuals or to the company, and try and grow that. Then underneath that is the mass. Try to have systems that control as much as you can. If you don't, they will do everything they can to make money out of you. That is the challenge. Every major company here is the same. And the bigger the business gets, the harder it gets. That's what we are working on.

II

Strategic plans meet Chinese reality

5

Disappointed expectations

During the 1980s and 1990s many companies went into China believing that the booming economy would provide a growing market. They were led in these assessments by hype from their own governments and the media about China's new 'market economy'. Most executives knew very little about China, which is understandable given that the country had been closed to the West for 30 years. Their advisers in legal and accountancy firms knew the black letter laws, issued in great abundance by the Chinese government, about how to structure investments and taxation, but not necessarily what it would actually be like to operate in China. An executive with a global company summed up his experience of the situation for business as: 'There is no blueprint.'

The strategic plans conceived at head office then had to be tested in the reality of the Chinese market. In the meeting between Western strategic plans and Chinese reality, Western directors, managers and technical experts suddenly found themselves in a situation they had not anticipated. The Chinese government, too, had oversold the opportunities for profit-making and hadn't undertaken detailed planning about how many international companies the market could support. So, while many Western companies were expecting that competition would be controlled by industry sector, in fact there were no controls and foreign companies crowded in. Companies then found they were but one player in an overcrowded market. It is not an exaggeration to say that shock, disbelief and anger were common responses, as documented in the following case study.

Case study: 'An absolute mirage'

The company in this case study is a consumer-goods manufacturer. Its board expected it would be one of twelve international manufacturers in its industry sector. After eight years in China the company is competing against 80 other international companies in Shanghai alone. The person giving this account is the head office executive responsible for China operations.

'China has played the greatest confidence trick of all time. In the 1980s they said, "Come in", and created a stampede. They convinced us to part with our hard-earned US dollars in cash. We took over essentially bankrupt and broke state enterprises. They said, "By the way, while you're at it, bring in your technology and train our employees".

'We are bringing in our technology, upgrading all the plants, training their employees, giving them pay rises, and at the same time they are using that information—because nothing stays a secret in China—to upgrade their own technology in the A-class and B-class enterprises in order to compete with us. They did it so successfully. We all charged in on the lure of this massive 1.2 billion market.

'Well, it's a mirage, an absolute mirage. There aren't 1.2 billion people who can afford to buy quality consumer goods. We are all struggling. Is it worth it? Maybe, if you've got a long-term view of it, and a long-term vision. But there is some pain to be had. The promises they made . . . it's a bureaucratic place, it's got hardships one has to endure. They are corrupt, too. You've always got to be watching. What is bred into them is a desire for bribery and corruption, which we found a bit hard to handle. But you've just got to put up with it.'

Contract defaulting

After the company established the joint venture, the Western executives discovered that their joint venture partners didn't have any money. They bought land for expansion which is now not worth the money they paid for it, but they can't sell it back. If they haven't developed it within the next few years the Chinese government will reclaim it.

The joint venture contract committed both partners to build a new plant. Part of the financing was to come from the Chinese partner. The foreign company had to negotiate to get the Chinese to put in their share of the money, but the Chinese partner wasn't prepared to do it. During negotiations the foreign partner spent time offering them incentives. With hindsight the foreign executive thinks he should have asked them, 'Do you have any money?' However, it's unlikely, he says, that they would have told him the truth about their situation.

He continued: 'The Chinese are inherent deal-makers. You don't know who is in charge, who is making the decisions. When we were negotiating the plant with our joint venture partner, he said, "I can't make these decisions because the Light

Industry Bureau makes them on our behalf". So we went to the Light Industry Bureau, and the person we talked to there said: "Well, it isn't me who is making the decisions; it's someone higher up." So we tried to identify who the "someone higher up" was who was making the decisions. It was constant buck-passing. We couldn't figure out who to talk to. And then they never tell you the truth, which was that they didn't have any money. They said things like, "We don't trust your figures", or "You don't have the figures set out the right way" or "You don't have the right contractor". All these sorts of things. In the end they didn't have any money. It became obvious to us after a while. Then we started asking a few more questions, like: "What other businesses are you connected with?" That might take three months of your working life. In our home market we are used to people having a common business ethic. We all operate by the same rules. If you say you'll do something, you do it. The opposite is true in China. They say something and it doesn't mean they will actually do it. That has been my experience.'

Contracts with retailers are equally open to variation. There are only about 1200 retail outlets that sell this company's product, and there are ten manufacturers all wanting to put up their signs on them. The rules are as follows.

'We go up and say, "We want to put our sign up there where you have that foreign brand sign". We say, "Well, how much are you getting for that sign?". And they say, "$1000 a month". We say, "Have we got a deal for you! We'll give you $3000 a month". They say, "Fine, thanks a lot".

'The retailer takes down the competitor's sign and throws it away, and puts up our sign. We send out four technicians to fix it properly and to take photos. Then the guy from another foreign company comes in and says, "That's a pretty good spot. You've got a new sign. How much are you getting for that?" "$3000." "OK, I'll give you $4000." So the retailer trashes our sign.

'We come back and say, "Hang on! We had a contract with you". He says, "Oh well, you didn't match the numbers. I'll give you a sign around the corner". And of course, if you try to take them to court, you're not going to get anywhere. In our home market, if they didn't hold to a contract we would threaten to take them to court. It's written in English, it's more understandable. People expect to be held to their word. Their word is their badge of honour. In China, breaking your word is seen to be acceptable.'

Private benefit

'I think they are self-centred from the business point of view: "It's profit for me, it's profit for my enterprise, it's profit so I can benefit"—and it's a lot more short term. The political leaders seem to have a long-term perspective, but business people are more: "What can I do today to benefit my company and my lot? And if it's going to cost me money in the short term to get a long-term benefit, then I don't want to do it!"'

The need for constant vigilance because of the Chinese concern for private benefit was brought home to the foreign executive in an incident with their distributors in southern China. The company had a marketing promotion in which customers could gain a monetary reward by returning to the company a winner's coupon hidden in some of the products. In the foreign company's home market the take-up rate on such a promotion would be 25–30 per cent. In China it was 100 per cent. When the expatriate executives investigated the situation they found that the distributors had opened every package, taken out the prize-winning coupons, resealed the product and sent it on to the retailers while pocketing the prize money themselves. The company's *own distributors* were undermining the company's reputation and relationship with the public, as well as cheating the manufacturer out of money.

The unlevel playing field

In addition to such unethical practices, there is a lot of competition from Chinese companies whose prices are lower and who don't have the financial burden of expatriate managers and their families. The company is forced to use expatriates to manage the business and improve the quality of packaging, services and products. Chinese brands are lower in quality and lower in price. The foreign product is 6 RMB, while Chinese brands are less than half the price: 1.6 or 2 RMB. The discriminating part of the market isn't growing at anything like the rate they expected it would. They have focused on the big cities, and that is where all the competition is: Japanese, Koreans, Taiwanese, Southeast Asians, Americans, Canadians, Europeans and Australians. For them to move to provincial markets would stretch their resources and would not be cost-effective.

This company sees China as an uneven playing field. The company started with tax breaks, but these have been extended to Chinese companies. The tax breaks are applied only when the company makes a profit, and his company hasn't yet made a profit. The Chinese tax authorities said to him, 'On the first half of your income you can pay minimal tax'. His response is, 'Well you've got to earn your income before you can pay minimal tax! We haven't done that yet'. The company is taxed on turnover. Even before his company has made any profit it has paid 30 per cent tax. At least, that is how he perceives the system working for foreign companies. He is not so sure that Chinese companies have to comply in this way.

Avoiding payment

The level of debt in China has affected his company, as it has so many others.

'Receivables are extraordinary. People don't pay. There is triangular debt. You go to your distributor and say, "You owe me some money". They say, "Well, the sub-distributor hasn't paid me, so when he pays me, I'll pay you". Then you ask the sub-distributor, who says: "Well, the sub-sub-distributor hasn't paid me, so when he pays me, I can pay the distributor, who can then pay you . . . ". We are the silly guys at the end of the line who haven't been paid. So they are all using our money, and we are financing the distribution system. It strings out as much as six months in comparison with our home market, which is seven days or pay on delivery. It's an expensive process.

'You think, "Gee, are we making any progress?" I don't think there are too many people whose experiences in China have been positive. If you are looking for pain, just look for a general manager in China.'

Comment

The head office perspective

It may seem that this executive has a highly exaggerated response to his company's experience in China. Business people who haven't had dealings in China may find this puzzling, and may dismiss it, saying: 'China can't be that bad!' Unfortunately, this executive is not alone in his assessment, as we shall see in the following three case studies. The majority of head office executives I interviewed for this book responded with a similar level of feeling, and drew on similar experiences to explain their position. Managers on the ground in China were not quite as emotive about their experiences. Although they had obstacles to surmount that were more difficult than in their home country experience, they generally described their experiences with less emotion. Obviously, they view the challenges as integral to their job, to be worked through and successfully dealt with. Some have found themselves in a losing battle and are resigned to it. One executive explained his situation by using a Chinese saying which means, 'A dead pig doesn't feel hot water.' But the head office executives are being judged on their strategic decision-making in relation to the international market, and thus have a greater sense of vulnerability in regard to the performance of their China investments. Therefore, their response is likely to be strong.

The managers who are located in China brought up the problem of head office expectations a number of times. One said: 'The board has to understand that it isn't an open invitation to make money. There is a lot of hard work to do. Things are difficult for head office to understand. Ours is a big company and they think that success should come to it automatically. But here it is different. China is a developing country, the economy is changing very rapidly and there is intense competition. It is a matter of giving head office some information about how the business is operating, and how Chinese people operate.'

China investments don't always represent a large percentage of a company's global business. If this is the case, it is more difficult for managers in China to obtain the support and time they need to effect an improved financial or market result. Many companies have scaled down their initial investments because they can't see that their strategic goals can be met in any reasonable time-frame.

Ethical differences

This case signals a series of issues that will be repeated in many of the case studies in this book. These are differing ethics governing business behaviour, particularly Chinese deception of Western partners, contract defaulting and non-payment of debt.

When human beings are shocked out of their normally accepted social world, they 'may take up a moral perspective to explain and control the ethical aspects of their troubles' (Kleinman 1988, pp. 27–28). It is obvious again and again in the interviews in this book that foreign executives dealing with China not only respond to problems with business strategies, but by interpreting their troubles in terms of ethics. Sometimes Chinese behaviour is interpreted as unethical because it doesn't obey the business rules that are accepted among business associates in the home market. In other cases, there is outright unethical behaviour. In this case study the executive singles out a number of aspects of the Chinese business scene as being unethical according to his standards.

He feels sold out by Chinese government officials who painted a rosy picture of the market and directed foreign investors towards their non-performing enterprises. He also objects to the Chinese government's policy of copying Western techniques in their own enterprises, thus providing strong competition in the marketplace. Of course, all companies scan the marketplace and learn from the products and processes of others. The Americans did it in the early twentieth century by copying European technology, and Japanese industry followed this path after the Second World War. Japanese industrial delegations visited leading US and European companies, and when they were not admitted, as in the case of the Scottish shipyards, they took photographs from outside the boundary fence. The Chinese, recognising how backward their industrial processes are, have naturally set out to learn from foreign companies. The executive in the case study is not used to government taking such an active role in business and standing behind the joint venture company's parent organisation.

Outrage is so noticeable among foreign executives that one wonders whether colonialist attitudes still influence Western attitudes to China. The Chinese certainly think so. At a conference in Beijing I heard the director of Shanghai Volkswagen criticising the Chinese authorities for opening the auto market to other foreign auto companies. His point was understandable, because Volkswagen has had to invest so much in technology and training to bring workers from bicycle technology to the technology level of the Volkswagen factory. Volkswagen's current return on investment, stated by the Chinese to be 13 per cent, was now in danger from other auto makers whose car designs are more advanced than the Shanghai 'Santana'. The German director spoke with the apparent assumption that his company had a right to Chinese government protection—not a point of view held by other international auto makers.

In the cool light of day, many reasons for moral outrage are simply commercial realities that are not exclusive to China. But there are other issues raised by the executive in the case study that are due to the particular nature of China. When the Chinese partner's lack of money to invest in the joint venture was disguised behind criticism of the Westerners' figures or procedures, the Westerners at first believed what they were being told, with the result that when they found out the truth it soured their perception of their partners and of the

Chinese in general. The Chinese disguised the negatives because they were desperate to get foreign investment. They used a typical Chinese technique of 'making something out of nothing' to divert the other side from the real issue. This is a classic tactic from Sunzi's *The Art of War*—just part of the way things work in China.

This case study shows how executives who are very successful and experienced in their home market, and other Western markets, can find themselves at sea in the cultural context of China. The communication, as described in Chapter 4, is indirect. It is probable that another Chinese person would have realised from the tactic used that the Chinese were hiding the real situation. The Westerners couldn't see that, because they expected straightforward and frank communication. In their thinking, the Chinese were their partners in a long-term investment. They were also associated with the government, another reason to trust them.

Although Westerners are more open to deception than business people of Chinese background, there are many overseas Chinese who believed the promises made to them by PRC partners and were severely disappointed. Most said nothing, because of the awful loss of face; they just abandoned their China investments. Lee Kuan Yew, the former Prime Minister of Singapore, launched an attack on the officials of Suzhou for their prevarication about building a 'mini Singapore' in that city, thus indicating that even the entrepreneurs of Singapore can have trouble with what is promised and what becomes reality with their ethnic brothers in China.

Debt and contract defaulting.

Used to a well-developed legal infrastructure to support commerce, Western executives have found it a hard transition to come to terms with the easy ability of Chinese customers to evade paying their debts and to breach contracts. Although China has maintained a high credit rating with international risk management agencies due to sovereign guarantees undertaken by the government, healthy foreign exchange reserves, stringent capital controls and a high national savings rate of 43 per cent of GDP, for companies operating in China's market who are unprotected by sovereign guarantees, debt is a serious management problem.

Contract defaulting is promoted by the highly competitive environment of China, as in the example of the advertising hoardings, and by the lack of dependable enforcement mechanisms for legal agreements. In Han China (206 BC to AD 220) and for centuries following, there were clauses in commercial contracts between people which said:

- 'Officials have government law and commoners have private contracts.'
- 'Officials have government law and do not accept private agreements as conclusive.'
- 'Officials have government, while the people have their own ways.' (Hansen 1995)

All indicate a reluctance by officials to involve themselves in contracts and contract litigation between ordinary people.

Little by little, strategies are developed by Western executives to deal with the realities of Chinese commercial life. In the case of debt, some companies will not supply goods until they are paid for. Others find flexible ways to be paid by a debtor company's associated businesses. Some will not supply a second consignment of goods until they receive payment for the previous consignment. Others use *guanxi* pressure and banquets, but this strategy is not always successful. Most just have to wear the debt. A powdered milk company in northern China which was issued with a huge tax bill told the local bureau that they would not be able to pay it because they hadn't been paid for their powdered milk by local enterprises. The Chinese authorities did a deal— the foreign company would pay the salaries of all the local teachers, because the county had no money to do so. This amounted to half the tax bill.   In return the remaining tax was cancelled. Flexibility is the key here.

For the executive in the case study, China has not so far been a good strategic investment. There is a multiplicity of problems, many deeply embedded in the Chinese context and effectively beyond the company's control. It is not surprising that the company has since sold the majority of its China investments.

6

Hidden agendas

In 1942 Mr A.V. Farmer, a director of the British chemical company ICI, had an interview with Chou Enlai. Chou, anticipating the communist victory in the civil war with the Nationalists, said: 'We shall be short of money, materials, technicians and traders. We will need the help of your company . . . Of course, eventually we will take over your property in China, your staff, your marketing facilities . . . ', which they did in 1953 (Brodie 1990, p. 214).

This attitude bears a close resemblance to that encountered by many Western executives in relations with their joint venture partners in the 1980s and 1990s. The Western business people expected trustworthy, co-operative business partners, since all were linked to government enterprises. They expected that together they would participate in the conversion of a state-controlled economy into a market economy. But Western executives discovered that their Chinese partner was concentrating on maximising its own gains from the partnership, especially since they were, in a strange echo of Chou Enlai's words, 'short of money, materials, technicians and traders'. The similarity in viewpoint is not surprising, given that in this case study, as in so many, the Chinese partners were Communist Party managers schooled for 30 years in anti-capitalist and anti-Western rhetoric. In

Hidden agendas 69

addition, state-owned enterprises were in deep financial trouble. In 1995 the debt to equity ratio was 570 per cent, and their bad loans to Chinese banks were estimated to be US$225 billion at the end of 1997.

Case study: 'It's war'

A manufacturer of industrial products operating in over twenty countries worldwide set up a manufacturing joint venture in Shanghai with the assistance of the Ministry of Foreign Trade and Economic Co-operation and other government ministries. Were they to establish themselves in China again, the head office executive responsible for China said they would not associate themselves with high-level government departments, but would come in 'under the radar' by splitting their investment into small parcels and avoiding publicity. In his estimation, the high-level linkages which were meant to unlock any door that was blocking progress on the project have meant only 'a weekly meeting with a whole bunch of bureaucrats who don't contribute anything'.

They were partnered with a very large government department, employing over 20 000 people, which was in the process of corporatisation. Their subsidy would soon disappear, and they had been instructed to manage their cost structure so that they would not continue to lose money.

Through the course of negotiating and setting up the joint venture business the attitude of the foreign executives changed from being reasonably clear-cut about what both parties were trying to do—set up a long-term, profitable and sustainable market share for their manufactured products—to realising that their Chinese partner's agenda was quite different from what they had thought it was.

What was driving the Chinese side was a short-term focus on profit and a lack of finance. The project had an initial investment of US$50 million, but the Chinese partner didn't have the cash to handle the start-up period. They disguised this in different ways. They tried to take money out of the joint venture to help fund their share; they forced the foreign partner to accept cheaper components in building the plant; and they tried to get commissions on all aspects of the construction and licensing processes. The Chinese partner would use any reason at all to prevent the foreign executives from seeing that they could not meet their financial obligation. The foreign executive described this experience.

'We didn't realise that they would disguise the real situation. It took six months for us to find out. We had a few concerns, but because the first expatriate general manager, a Malaysian Chinese, was compromising and hiding it from head office it wasn't so apparent. But the more defensive of their position they became, not letting us know what the real position was, the more aggressive they became, and the less the initial warm feelings we had about them became sustainable. Eventually you don't have a relationship, you just have a fight, and it's very difficult to go back from that point. I don't know too many joint ventures that have reached the bottom and come up again.'

Commissions

One issue that caused on-going conflict was that the Chinese partner saw it as legitimate for them to take a gain out of building the factory, whereas the foreign partner saw it as a conflict of interest. The Chinese attempted to take a commission on all activities. Sometimes the commission was up-front, but more often it was done without the knowledge of the foreign side—'through the back door'.

The Chinese position was that they wanted all construction contracts to go to the construction divisions of their parent company. When the foreign company insisted on giving contracts to the contractors best qualified to undertake the work, the Chinese side wanted to take a commission from them. Without informing the foreign partner, the Chinese partner's senior management, including the president, would visit contractors chosen by the foreign side and instruct them to increase their price so that they could pay them a commission. They would threaten contractors, saying: 'Unless you can give a commission, we'll make sure you don't get the contract.' It affected every aspect of the setting-up, including telephone access and water supply contracts. The foreign executives believed such actions were not only directed to benefiting the Chinese parent company, but the Chinese directors as individuals. The foreign executives dubbed it 'The Supplementary Retirement Fund'. An executive describes the problems this hidden agenda caused in the joint venture board.

'We couldn't sign a contract above a certain amount without board agreement. So they had opportunities to reject things in that way. They continually raised issues like, "This is an infringement of Chinese law". We would then spend a lot of time ensuring that we weren't in fact breaking Chinese law, and usually we weren't. They set up blocks. When a signature was needed, they delayed it. They just dragged it out and dragged it out. They would do that on a major contract in order to get a concession in their favour on a minor contract.'

In order to pacify the Chinese directors, the foreign directors agreed to their demands for local Chinese contractors to be used on some contracts. What the Western executives feared would happen, did. Although the local contractors knew the specifications stipulated in the contracts, they tried to maximise their returns by cutting back on quality. This led to forced rework, sometimes up to five times because when doing the rework they also cut corners. Whole areas of steel fabrication had to be taken away, and pipes already laid and encased in concrete had to be dug up and re-laid because the contractors had not followed the directive that they were to be laid in plastic.

When the foreign partner wanted to use their own engineering group from overseas for quality control and experience in building a state-of-the-art plant, their partners accused them of increasing the cost of the project by paying the project engineering group 'excessive fees'. The executive said, 'They accused us of doing what they do! In other words, they were convinced we were ripping them off because we had an in-company group doing project managing. That's the way they operate themselves.'

Arguments about the payment went on for a year. 'They were peeved because this group wouldn't give them free rein. It was part of a concerted effort to get it changed. They wouldn't agree to paying the fees to the overseas project managers. We just said that it's not a board-approved decision. It doesn't have to have board approval. So we went ahead and made the payments, which upset them. The Chinese fought that tooth and nail, saying it should be a local company. They were perfectly happy to have the joint venture pay one of their companies the same amount—more than happy. That was their deliberate campaign. In the joint venture agreement it was agreed that this overseas contracting group would be appointed. But that's one of those things they agree to on joint venture signing; it's another to live with it afterwards.'

Getting government approvals was an opportunity for the Chinese partner to earn money from the foreign company. When a licence for power was needed, the Chinese partner tried to set themselves up as the conduit to the Chinese government bureau which issued approvals. They objected strongly when the foreign partner went direct to the power bureau, saying: 'We're the Chinese partner, so our role should be to manage the Chinese relationships. Yours is to bring the technology and build the plant. If we tell you it is 1 million RMB to get xyz licence, then that's what it is.' The foreign executive replied, 'Well no, it isn't. Our information is that the fee is only half that. Who is getting the other half of that?' This caused them to get really upset.

Unfair tactics

The head office executive found that the first general manager, a Malaysian Chinese project engineer, had allowed the Chinese partner to re-negotiate the original terms on the land price and was making concessions which head office wasn't aware of, in order to get co-operation. He was dismissed by the foreign partner and replaced by a very experienced China-hand, married to a local, who had started up joint ventures before.

The boardroom became a battleground. The head office executive said: 'The partner went all out to break the new GM through victimisation. They employed every method to apply pressure— such as procrastination. He needed a decision made, a contract signed, so they just kept asking questions, slowing him down. In board meetings, they caused him to lose face by not acknowledging him in the meeting. They would argue about things and bring in a whole pile of law books to support their stand. They would write letters demanding information, and when it had been provided, write the same letters a couple of months later for the same information. When he didn't co-operate in some areas, they wrote to me (Head of Asian Operations), and when I wouldn't co-operate, they would write to the CEO.

'It was just escalation of pressure. They were vocally very aggressive, particularly one of the directors—a bully, cunning and dominating. They threatened to blow up the general manager's car. The partners were middle-aged; they had come through the Cultural Revolution, and had their brief from their board. It was just a standard "extract anything you can get out of the joint venture" mentality. Very aggressive. They didn't have a clue about business. What they were expert in was negotiating, in being able to screw you down to the last cent, and in how to be so difficult that they would cause people to give in.'

At board meetings the Chinese would tell the foreign executive he was not respecting them: 'You do not show respect.' In his eyes they were often extremely insulting to him, pouring scorn on detailed research that recommended a way of handling the business different from that wanted by the Chinese partner. They would also say, 'You don't understand how to conduct business here'. One example was the recruitment process. The Western partner researched how much they would need to pay to get the right people. The Chinese side wanted to transfer people from their organisation and told the Western executives at great length that they didn't know what they were doing, that their approach was wrong. The foreign general manager brought in an employee from outside Shanghai without clearing the paper chain that allows an employee to leave one employer and move to another. The Chinese partner reported it to the Labour Bureau and the joint venture was fined. They negotiated their way out of the fine eventually. The Chinese partners made a big issue of it, saying: 'You don't know the rules. You must let us do it. You don't understand. You don't know anything about it.'

Contract defaulting

Although the price of the land had been agreed to, the Chinese partners later wanted to renegotiate it. They brought in other related issues to reopen negotiations. The executive said, 'It was just another front. It's war, and they just open fronts and force you to fight on so many fronts that you will lose on some, like playing the odds.

'They agreed to so many things that they reneged on later. One of the conditions of the purchase of the land was that it was to be completely cleared of any obstruction. We especially wanted the land to have no people on it, so we got that, but it had two old army concrete pill boxes and the remains of a factory. We had an enormous problem getting the Chinese partner to carry out their agreement about clearing the land. They hadn't told us that they had no prior approval to move the pill boxes. Eventually it got to the point that I stopped the project. I said to them, "We will walk away from this unless you get them moved, because it will jeopardise the operation of the plant". I went to the site manager and told him to start demobilising everyone, knowing they would be back in half an hour flat. We got them moved.

'To get anything done required that degree of confrontation. It was just a continual fight to get them to do what they'd agreed to, because it cost money. So they procrastinate, knowing that if we are to keep on schedule we will do it. You give an inch, they take a mile.'

Avoiding payment

While the plant was being built the Western executives formulated a plan to build market share using imported product. Both sides agreed that the foreign parent company would sell some product directly to large projects, and not go through a distribution channel. The Chinese partner's parent company was a distributor of finished products. They wanted to be the channel through which the market opening products were sold. After long discussion, both sides agreed that the Chinese partner would sell to small accounts, and the foreign side directly to bigger accounts.

The foreign company had a policy that all imports into China were by Letters of Credit, which meant they were paid for. The Chinese directors said, 'We are your partners—surely you trust us to be part of this market development?

If we are to stock the warehouse and have good services, we need some terms.'

The foreign directors originally said no. Eventually they agreed that the Chinese partner would get terms whereby they paid 30 days ex-warehouse, but the warehouse stock remained the possession of the foreign partner up to the point of sale. The Chinese got a credit for the stock that they sold. The Chinese director absolutely guaranteed there was no way they would renege on that. And within the first 30 days they reneged.

The Chinese deputy general manager knew the prices quoted on the direct sale accounts. He took that pricing information, then quoted lower to sell from his distribution outlet and took the terms beyond the agreed 30 days in order to close the sales. He was effectively getting the foreign partner to subsidise having stock in China in order for him to sell on extended terms and at a cheaper price.

The foreign partner continuously brought up the non-payment. The Chinese directors would deny it, or say it was 'special circumstances', or 'it was your fault because it was late' or 'it was broken'. To the foreign executives it seemed that the excuses were 'whatever came into their heads'. In the end, the only way they got paid was by deducting the amount from the price they eventually paid to buy out the joint venture partner.

Joint venture to wholly-owned enterprise

Under the new foreign general manager, things changed. He had experience, and he had friends in the Chinese bureaucracy who undermined some of the implied authority of the Chinese partner.

He was able to use his contacts in the bureaucracy to say, 'Well, that's not right'.

Eventually the foreign partner decided to buy out the Chinese side and establish a wholly-owned foreign invested enterprise. One of the Chinese directors on the board was blamed by the Chinese joint venture partner for the disintegration of the relationship. He was moved to another department. The other director was forced into retirement. The acquisition was handled by Chinese government departments responsible for relationships with foreign companies, in an effort to minimise the bad publicity and loss of face on the Chinese side.

Assessing his experiences, the foreign director said, 'There is a Shanghainese element as distinct from a Chinese element. In the south we had negotiated a preliminary agreement on a joint venture but we ended up deciding not to go ahead with it. That was a huge loss for the particular town, to the mayor of the township, the mayor of the province, every level through Guangdong. Over quite a long period we talked to them about the problem and did a lot of research into why, in the end, it wouldn't work. It was a very amicable parting.

'I think in Shanghai they are much more aggressive, more ruthless, argumentative. It's not a win–win situation. If you are left with something, they have lost. There isn't the type of negotiation where you want a satisfactory outcome for both sides. Everything has to be argued about. Our experience of our partners was that it was plain opportunistic greed. It has been an enormous distraction. It has slowed the project down and been very frustrating. It has cost us about US$1 million dollars.'

Comment

Different agendas

In both case studies so far in this part we have been dealing with Chinese partners who don't have the funds to finance their investment in the joint venture. It is arguable that it was a deliberate strategy of the Chinese government to attract foreign investment and for the bureaucrats handling negotiations to disguise their inability to fund their agreed equity share. Reports of this occurrence go back to the first joint ventures of the early 1980s. Many Chinese have the view that foreign companies are rich, so they can pay. The Chinese side in this case study wanted to make money and to retain money in their associated companies, and they were prepared to go to any lengths to achieve that goal. For the Western partner it was a matter of building a state-of-the-art plant and setting up the business on accepted Western business principles.

The Chinese partner, being a very big enterprise with supply, manufacturing and marketing arms, was used to using their muscle to achieve their ends. They came up against a very big Western company, equally committed to running the business according to their own criteria. In this and the previous case study, because of Chinese debt and partner disputes, the foreign companies decided to buy out the Chinese partner's equity share in the joint venture and continue the business as a wholly-owned enterprise.

There is a certain vindictiveness in the Chinese perception of Western companies. It was fostered by the 'hundred years of humiliation' following the Opium Wars and also the anti-foreign, anti-capitalist propaganda of the communist period. The highly competitive tactics in this case study demonstrate how such perceptions are carried through into action to a degree unanticipated by foreign executives. In another joint venture the foreign executives were enjoying a pleasant lunch to celebrate the opening of the joint venture. One of the foreign executives had been slow in transferring US$2 million to China, a part of the foreign equity investment. The senior Chinese negotiator turned around and said, with hatred in his voice, 'If that investment hasn't arrived by tomorrow, the foreign side will get *nothing!*' In this remark he showed the mental divide that demarcates foreigners from the Chinese.

Later in this book, in the section on foreign managers and Chinese staff, there is evidence of anti-foreign attitudes and actions, as well as extreme sensitivity about the way foreigners speak to the Chinese, illustrated in this case study by the charge, 'You do not show respect.'

Stereotypes and bad practice

The foreign executive in this case study is at pains to point out that he does not believe all Chinese behave as his joint venture partners did. He experienced a different relationship in south China. It is important when reading these case studies that we do not stereotype all Chinese people in business. However, as these case studies document, bad practice is more often the case at present, than good. In contemporary China, afflicted by severe debt, a free-for-all regulatory environment and an immense desire to get rich following the commercial repression of the communist period, unscrupulous and unethical practice is commonly encountered. Executives used to the regulated environment of the advanced Western economies simply cannot assume that the Chinese share their experience or outlook.

There is a case to be made that highly competitive behaviour is a natural feature of the Chinese business tradition. Chinese business people have never had a strong commercial legal infrastructure to support good practice or to penalise defaulters. Prior to the communist period, Chinese business people sought associates through recommendation or through the guilds. These methods were important ways to control a person's involvement with unscrupulous business people. A Chinese small businessman explained it by saying: 'We make a point of passing on information about who are our old friends. Then the connections show up. It's a referral system. You need to know the person well enough so that you won't lose face by referring him on. That is where *guanxi* and face come together.'

The Chinese company's desire to keep all contracts within their group was because they were under pressure to make money and there was a government policy to enforce localisation in materials purchase, contracting and staff recruitment. However, taking commissions is a time-honoured commercial practice in China. The Western criteria, 'the best contractor for the job', is less common than using related contractors or in-house contractors who pay a percentage to the go-between.

Chinese contractors are closely associated through a contracting pyramid. A job is contracted to a certain company, who sub-contracts it to another company and so on for as many as seven sub-contractors. Each company takes a percentage off the contract price, with the result that the contractor doing the job is being paid a fraction of the original contract price, and he gives quality accordingly—if he even knows what the original specifications were.

When Chinese in the early twentieth century observed the relations between Western companies they could not believe how loose they were. A member of a Chinese guild commented, 'The resolution that held them together was like a ligature of sand' (MacGowan 1886, p. 166). The tradition was for Chinese businesses to belong to guilds which provided co-operative networks of long-term business relationships. The guilds formed vertical monopolies over goods and services. The guilds fixed minimum prices and put non-members out of business by boycotting them and coercing their employees. As long as the guild had a monopoly, non-guild members could only operate on the guild's terms. There was no commercial court system to enforce agreements. The guilds provided the networks and power to lower the risk in commercial agreements.

Such arrangements have been duplicated in the monopolies of the socialist period, the Chinese partner in this case study being one of the largest. The same pattern of tight linkages and monopoly organisations is evident in most Asian countries. In Japan are the *keiretsu*, in Korea the *chaebol* and in Southeast Asia the overseas Chinese family-owned conglomerates.

I do not want to suggest that what occurred in the case study is a wholly acceptable and defensible behaviour in the Chinese context. Rather, there are customary methods of conducting business, such as the taking of commissions, that are different from in the advanced Western economies. Researchers of the fortunes of British businesses in China from the mid-nineteenth century to the 1930s noted that British companies were generally 'beaten by the Chinese game: the ability of the Chinese to survive and their willingness to persevere on . . . the 2½ per cent margin' (MacPherson and Yearley 1987). Overlaid on this is that in business between Chinese and foreigners, the Chinese may well say, 'This is our country—why should we tell the foreigners what we are doing?' This is not a good basis for a long-term commercial relationship, but it is one commonly encountered by foreign companies in China.

7

Corrupt practices

An issue for foreign executives is the degree to which they participate in the culture of corruption and facilitation. Some see facilitation payments and services as the equivalent of sponsorship, public relations, marketing and advertising in the developed markets of the West. If a company, to gain a licence, is asked to invest US$100 000 or $500 000 in a venture unrelated to their business, is this corruption? If the licence depends on it, is it avoidable?

Big companies have staff dedicated to fostering relations with the bureaucracy, but these staff always run the risk of being on the other side of the law. A number of Chinese background employees of multinational companies have been arrested and imprisoned on corruption charges.

Chinese background employees feel the weight of customary practice in China, and may, unknown to their foreign employers, respond to local pressures. When they need bureaucratic help, they have to provide incentives to obtain it. What is most in short supply in China is enough upright and incorruptible officials.

With so much bad practice at the top levels of the bureaucracy, it is understandable that private benefit through sharp practices flourishes further down the ladder. Theft of property, 'the squeeze' and other illicit activities provide a source of finance and materials for enterprising employees in an environment of extreme shortage.

All these levels of corrupt practices provide challenging scenarios for foreign executives, as illustrated in the following case study.

Case study: 'That's the way it works'

The subject of this case study is the head office managing director of a telecommunications manufacturer with production facilities in both north and south China, and a marketing network into all provinces. He has had to deal with a steady stream of incidents relating to corrupt practices. All his customers are government departments.

'There is no relationship between price and cost. The entertaining and the deals that are done by the Chinese are more extensive than foreign-owned joint ventures are prepared to go to. In Chinese organisations the culture is to look after your customers or potential customers with the banquets, *maotais* and all that stuff. The customers expect it. That's the way it works.'

In one of his factories in north China the Chinese general manager and a Malaysian Chinese financial controller used 800 000 RMB, without permission from head office, to buy a Mercedes 560 SEL from the United States to give to a senior Chinese official. They used the company money to buy the car and bring it into the country, but then the official decided he didn't want it. They had it in the factory for six months. Every time the foreign managing director went to China, they would shift the car into the street until he'd gone, then they would put it back in the factory compound. When he found out about it he went to China and fired both of them. The company sold the car, dropping US$50 000– 60 000 on the sale. The financial controller went on to work as commercial director for a European company. The Chinese deputy general manager was forced into retirement amid a sustained campaign of opposition from his former bureau colleagues who wanted their 'old comrade' reinstated.

Private benefit

After that he appointed a Malaysian Chinese to a new post of both financial controller and general manager. The new general manager uncovered that illegal deals were being done by the Chinese operations manager. When he tried to stop them, the operations manager organised local Chinese workers in a revolution against him. He phoned the managing director at head office because he thought he was going to be killed. The managing director immediately flew to China accompanied by an ex-SAS commander to protect him. The factory was in disarray. All the workers wore bandannas tied around their heads, and had hung long banners denouncing all Western imperialists around the factory walls. The atmosphere was violent. One of the ringleaders smashed a large plate glass coffee table as he tried to take on the managing director. The Public Security Bureau was called in and they arrested the ringleaders who all came from a little town nearby. The managing director made a statement about the experience:

'I think this kind of thing has always been going on in China and is not just a consequence of the Cultural Revolution. The insistence by the partner on having the deputy general manager as one of their people is to ensure that the local Chinese don't forget the political message, which in many cases is counter-productive to Western management techniques. I think there is underlying disquiet in all of these joint ventures. All the Chinese are in it for what they can get. They see it as a gravy train.'

Most recently one of their former agents and a woman from the Ministry of Foreign Trade and Economic Co-operation (MOFTEC) were arrested by the authorities for taking commissions from facilitation work. The agent was sentenced to fourteen years' gaol, the MOFTEC official to life imprisonment.

The company is now trying to recover US$1 million from their previous sales manager in south China who was running contracts through a company owned by his wife. This is proving to be a difficult assignment because his aunt is at a high level in an internal security division of government. His wife had their son in the US in order to make him eligible for a foreign passport.

At the other end of the scale, a low-level clerk embezzled US$40 000 over five years by falsifying petty cash dockets or changing the amount on cheque stubs. The Public Security Bureau was called in and her family is being given the opportunity to repay it. For some time the company had very high motor vehicle expenses because the driver and the local repairer had a deal. They used false invoices and were splitting the profits.

This company experienced pressure to conform to local business practices. 'One of the issues for us is that because we are a public company with corporate governance and all those sorts of things, we play it absolutely by the book on all of our importing. All of our copper is imported—we pay the tax, we just want to be clean, we don't want to be nailed. Our competitors, whether they are state-owned enterprises or Hong Kong joint ventures, smuggle copper in through Vietnam, and the military control all the import–export licences on the coast, particularly in the south, and deals are done. We actually come under pressure from time to time from agents who say, "If you don't import your copper through us, your shipments will be delayed". And when you dig deep into who is this agent, who is supporting him, it will be some branch of the military.'

Competition

The telecommunications products the company manufactures are over-supplied in China. In 1989 there was no capacity and each of the provinces was competing for who could get the most foreign investment. A plan issued from Beijing specified the number of telephone lines to be installed in a province. So, state-owned organisations saw the opportunity to vertically integrate and make profits. A Chinese bank would underwrite the loan. The Chinese directors would get on a plane and go and talk to all the foreign machinery vendors. They would be wined and dined extensively and come to an agreement. If they had done a deal worth US$10 million, they would say, 'Send us the invoice for $11 million', and $1 million goes to the people doing the business. This executive considers that the factory managers were buying plant and equipment simply because it was a way to pick up extra cash from the machinery manufacturers.

So much plant and equipment has been imported there is now huge overcapacity. A third of the manufacturers are foreign-invested joint ventures, another third are Chinese companies with a technology transfer agreement with a foreign company, and then another third are state-owned enterprises who have put in plant and equipment. Because of the overcapacity the pricing and profit margins are low. Added to this are serious problems with debt repayment.

'Without any doubt at all our biggest problem is getting paid for what we've delivered. My accounts receivable are at about 250 days. So my debtors are out at nine months, when we have one-month trading terms. I can send people to sit outside a customer's door for the cheque, and we've tried a percentage off in a brown paper bag to get our cheque. We've done everything we can to get paid. Threatening legal action is just a waste of time.'

Because of these developments the foreign managing director says, 'For our company, being in China isn't profitable. I'm rooted and I can't get out. It would cost me too much money to close it up. If I liquidated the business I would take a huge loss on assets, so I'm better off losing half a million per plant than taking a US$10 million hit. I want out. The reality is that we will never be able to make any money there. If you look at the real, real cost of doing business there . . . we reported profits in the early years, but the reality is that we didn't make any money there. It was all about opportunity. On paper it made good sense. But we spent no time looking at how we would run the business once we'd invested our money.'

Comment

Here we get a sense of the excess it is possible to run up against in contemporary China. There is no doubt it can be frightening.

Entertaining and 'face-giving'

For Chinese businessmen, looking after business or government associates requires a lavish banquet, which could include excessive drinking and toasting, followed by karaoke and even call girls. In the current environment, where the businessmen are either using state-owned enterprise money or their own company's tax-free profits, the expenses incurred are well compensated for in the deals agreed to. Lavish entertainment is a sign of status and affluence in a society where many have been traditionally living in poverty.

Not all Western executives are negative about the banqueting scene. Some have found entertainment to be beneficial in reaching their desired goals. When one foreign company found that their Chinese joint venture partner couldn't fund their share of the initial investment, a head office executive asked a contact in CITIC to assist. That contact knew a former four-star general who had once worked for the government bureau to which the Chinese partner reported. The CITIC contact and the general were engaged on US$4000 per day to hold high-level meetings and banquets with bureau officials. They were to tell them that their subsidiary didn't have any money, and to talk them into lending the subsidiary US$2 million. If not, the foreign partner would pull out of the joint venture. They spent four days on this mission in Shanghai and the deal was done. About one month later the money arrived and the joint venture could continue. Many executives accept the banquet and karaoke entertainment as a way to negotiate through problems.

Expensive imported cars signal power and business

success. The president of a Chinese construction company, wanting to establish his credibility with potential Western associates, sent his representative to see them. He showed them photos of the president's six cars, Cadillac, Mercedes, BMW . . . and photocopies of the registration documents.

No doubt the gift of a Mercedes seemed like an effective strategy to the two Chinese executives in the case study. Their problem was that they misjudged what was permissible for head office, and that was that the business be run according to the company's transparent accountability standards.

Although the government and the Public Security Bureau are committed to fighting these excesses, it is a difficult task when government officials and managers of public organisations are participants. Because of official involvement in corrupt activities, getting justice through local officials proved to be a long and difficult process in a number of criminal offences against overseas Chinese. In one case, Taiwanese tourists were robbed and then drowned when their tourist launch was deliberately set on fire and sunk. In another case a Southeast Asian businessman was robbed and had his throat slit while taking a taxi from Chengdu airport to the city. China is no longer the controlled society Westerners experienced in the communist period.

In this case study the foreign managing director used the local Public Security Bureau to solve his problems with the local criminals. He also used them with the clerk who embezzled US$40 000. Other companies have reported effective assistance from the Public Security Bureau in blackmail and ransom cases.

Because of the significance of entertainment in facilitation, large Western companies have facilitation departments, the so-called government co-ordination departments. Some Western executives explain it as the Chinese equivalent of advertising and promotional marketing. But the work can be hazardous. Facilitators tread a fine line between legitimacy and criminality. The power bases of officials can change, as in this case study where their former agent and his MOFTEC contact were arrested and imprisoned. When crackdowns occur, multinational companies close down the activities of their government co-ordination departments, thus indicating the grey area in which they work.

Debt and getting paid

This executive has found the brown paper bag method of debt collection unrewarding. Other foreign executives have found 'local methods' don't necessarily work. The following comment is from an executive in Beijing.

'I've come to believe less in *guanxi* and more in a sound commercial basis to the business. All the *guanxi* in the world won't get you payment unless you have a strong commercial basis. Originally we started with presents, trips, dinners. We begged, we pleaded, we paid them money under the table—all sorts of things to try and get money out of them. We've taken legal action. That is a particularly useless course of action because they don't care. The structure is orientated towards them and they know it. We've won court cases to have money paid to us, but we see no action because they change the legal entity of the business, or transfer the money into another account and say, "I have no money to pay. You can see for yourself the accounts for that business. It is bankrupt". We say, "Last week you transferred the money into another account". Our legal threats have fallen on deaf ears.

'They won't pay if they can avoid it. They said to our sales manager, "I would rather kill my brother than not pay you". And then the next week they didn't pay. I wouldn't trust anything they say about their willingness to pay on any commercial transaction. We now take a less diplomatic approach. We will not supply product unless they pay us first, or we get payment from them before we give them another order. We've been bitten severely by people promising us things and then not delivering.'

Other companies have been paid by a kind of 'counter-trade'. One manufactures vehicle components. When they supply product to the Chinese manufacturer of the vehicle, he cannot pay them. The payment is made by the retail sales company when the vehicles are sold.

In the old days, before the communist revolution, Western business had to contend with conditions not so different from today, where everyone was out to make a profit for themselves and 'business ethics' didn't count for much. ICI (China) found that when they increased prices, most of their Chinese agents, scattered over the length and breadth of China, reported back that all their stocks were sold. They then sold their unsold stocks at the new price, reporting at the lower price to ICI and pocketing the difference. Sales increased dramatically when prices were increased and declined when prices were reduced. They returned damaged stock for replacement first, after the price increase was announced. They thus made a profit while ICI (China) sustained losses (Brodie 1990, p. 144).

ICI supplied their agents in south China on cash or very short-term credit and their agents in north and central China with extended credit. However, when trading conditions were unfavourable, credit terms were withdrawn everywhere (Brodie 1990, p. 101).

A report on customary practices from the 1930s states that wholesalers expected 90 days' credit from foreign manufacturers. The Chinese wholesaler would extend 30 days' credit to reliable retailers and sell for cash to hawkers and small dealers. The wholesaler would then lend the 60 days' credit he had in hand as a banker, in small amounts at high interest. With this income he could finance a chain of retail shops or more wholesale establishments (Crow 1937). In the 1800s, Chinese businesses granted one another credit until the next customary settling day: in June, September and February, which was Chinese New Year, without regard to when the goods were provided. One of the early ICI executives, Henry Glendinning, reported to head office in 1899 that, 'The foreign merchants do not do this . . . that is one difficulty . . . to consumers buying . . . from foreigners' (Brodie 1990, p. 20).

Overcapacity

This case study has brought us full circle to the underlying financial problems of many Western-invested enterprises in China: the overcapacity for the market, competition not only with other foreign companies but with local companies. This has dealt a blow to the expectations of these foreign executives and made a nonsense of the strategic plans upon which they premised their investment in China.

This managing director concludes his account with the sobering forecast that profitability for his company is not an achievable goal. Considerations about the company's reputation in their head office market are keeping it in China. The seeds for this scenario were laid at the very beginning of the strategic planning. As he said, 'We spent no time looking at how we would run the business once we'd invested our money'.

8

Trust

Trust is based on shared values. It is as much about law and contract as it is about reciprocity, moral obligation and duty towards the community (Fukuyama 1995). Since Westerners and their parent organisations are not integral parts of the Chinese community where values and goals are shared and where obligations have been built up over a long time-frame, they are not included in the Chinese community of trust. This opens the way for duplicity in the treatment of the outsider.

Over half of all foreign investors now select a wholly-owned structure rather than a joint venture. This is a solution to lack of trust between partners. However, it is not always possible to dispense with partners. This is so in the next case study. It comes from a large global company in the wine and spirits industry who established a joint venture with four Chinese partners to grow and process grapes for wine and spirit production for the Chinese market. They had formerly had a very successful business exporting to China. Here the head office executive responsible for China discusses his experience of the issue of trust in working with his company's Chinese partners.

Case study: 'Sitting on nothing'

'With four partners there are a lot of things going on behind the scenes. They joke all the time, they laugh all the time. It's always wonderful and they challenge each other—it's great fun. But sometimes they are more mean than they sound. They don't show their emotions. They are a secretive civilisation. Sometimes you wonder that if they have been thinking in one direction for so long, perhaps they don't see things as we do.'

Of over 100 people in the Chinese company, he trusts only a few people in China. Two are in Hong Kong on the international board. They are driving the venture. His company controls 51 per cent of the joint venture equity. He believes that if you have less than 51 per cent it is 'a long-term waste of time'. His reason is, 'because you are dealing with persons who have known very hard times, who have been kept in China, who have been kept without freedom for a very long time'. In other words, people who are Sino-centric, who will put their needs above those of the joint venture.

He is forthright on the issue of trust. To illustrate his thinking he gave an example from his experience in China.

'One year we had a wine press coming from overseas. That press was unloaded, put on to a truck which left the port for the five- to six-hour journey to the winery. One hundred metres away from the ship was a concrete bridge. The container wouldn't fit under the bridge—it hit the bridge and bent the structure. We now know that the people at the winery, the customs and the transport company knew that they had broken the press just as it was leaving the port. As soon as they knew it a big banquet was organised, a big celebration. So when the press arrived at the vineyard, yes, there was a problem, but they thought they wouldn't worry about it until the next morning. That was ten days before vintage, so it was a serious problem. We left the banquet about midnight. The problem was covered up by everyone because they were all covering for each other. Why? There wasn't one who had the guts to try and claim the insurance because they would have to point out who had made a mistake. So they all lied to us.'

The investigation

'The investigation took us six months. We tested the concrete on the bridge and the concrete that was in the press, and it was the same. They said, "When the press arrived and we opened the container the press was broken". I said, "Alright, I've never seen any concrete in a container before". They were afraid. But they thought that the easiest way was to get money and compensation from outside China. OK, the press is broken. The only ones who are going to pay are the supplier of the press or the shipping company that transported it from Europe to Shanghai. They don't want the Chinese harbour authorities to have anything to do with it. They don't want the local transporter who is contracted between the port authorities and our own people to be questioned. It's all too hard. They don't want any kind of problem. And they would lie and lie and lie. The cover-up went on and on, where people lie in front of you.

'We proved it at meetings where the facts were there and they were still denying them, saying, "We don't know what happened". You can't push

it too much. Then what do you do? Fire everybody
and close the plant? They know that you are not
a fool, but you should never tell them, "You told
me lies for six months". If you do that you have
lost face, their authority has been questioned,
their leadership has been damaged and they are
going to hate you to death. This is why a lot of
people talk about the losing face thing. Everything
is a constant test of strength. In those challenges
you've got to make sure that even if there is a
winner, the winner is never declared, but everybody remembers what happened, and that's what
is keeping the system going. And if you don't show
strength they won't respect you either.

'They thought that by having the banquet we
wouldn't pursue the problem. *No one* would pursue
it. They thought even the people in our company
wouldn't care about it. There was really a sense
that it's all too hard; nobody wants to hear anything about it. That is when you are in trouble.
If once you thought you could trust a person, that
is when you discover that you are sitting on
nothing.

'You have to be on the ground 24 hours a day,
speaking Chinese, to keep everybody on the line.
Why did the winery manager get tangled with
the others? He must owe a lot of favours to the
customs people. Is he related to the owners of
the transport company? Was the truck driver the
brother of the local mayor? It can be a lot of
things. There was a very good reason for the
winery manager to take the position that the press
was broken by no one in China. And this is why
we never really blamed him for it. But he understood very clearly that this was a one-off thing,
and whatever his position, he is the manager and
he should be strong enough to be respected

through the chain of things. A lot of things are like that. Doing business is not all nice and friendly and kissing, and that sort of thing. Everything isn't *win win win* when you are in a joint venture with four different parties. Things can be done in China, but the only way you can have real satisfaction is to be very prudent. If you send a twenty-year-old, unless he is exceptional he is going to go head-on there, and he's going to be exploited, abused and used.'

The settlement

The problem of the press was settled to the satisfaction of both sides. The supplier flew over another press, and for the next eighteen months the foreign company got favours from the customs on the importation of goods. The company paid all the bills, but the compensation from the customs matched the costs. After eighteen months they were in the black.

'You have to show strength,' the foreign manager commented, 'in that you have to tell them, "Alright, we are going to have an investigation guys. This is how an investigation takes place . . . ". For that three months you will see false documents, false declarations, one after another. You challenge them, you say, "Well look, see this date in Chinese—this report was done three months after the date the press was unloaded. I don't think that document is really relevant". They know very well what that means, that the documents aren't going to stack up when you have an international organisation coming to investigate concerning the recovery of funds.

'They keep coming with fakes and you say, "I want a report showing what was stated, to find

out who said that". They say, "Yes, fair enough".
But what they give you isn't the document that
you want. They can produce anything you want.
And they can change the dates, or change the
stamps. They are professional liars.'

Comment

Honesty and deception

Westerners who haven't worked in China may be shocked
by the opinions of the winery executive and by his relentless
pursuit of where responsibility lay for the damage to the
wine press. But this is often the behaviour forced on
Western executives by the position they find themselves in
in China. His own opinion is that China is 'a secretive
civilisation'. Colourful as his description is, it points to the
Chinese custom of keeping damaging information to themselves. Theirs is not the open, problem-solving approach
expected by Western joint venture partners of their Chinese
partners.

This secretiveness about Chinese actions and agendas
has come up a number of times in the case studies. I
don't want to suggest that Western companies never
indulge in secretiveness where financial penalties are
involved, but complaints about Chinese secretiveness are
so common among Western companies in joint ventures
with Chinese enterprises that due weight should be given
to the management problems these create. In this case,
spending valuable foreign exchange from joint venture
reserves to buy and transport another wine press from
Europe if they admitted fault was a powerful disincentive
to the group about being honest about the situation. The
tactic of the banquet was calculated to 'stuff the mouths'
(*tianzui*) of the foreigners so that they would be rendered
silent on the matter. It was a tactic to invoke reciprocity.
This same pressure has been exerted on overseas Chinese

general managers, and the Western head office has found out belatedly that the manager has succumbed (see Chapters 6 and 7).

It is a common observation that Chinese staff are skilled at telling Western managers what what they want to hear, rather than the truth, and at fabricating illogical excuses in problem situations. There are a number of explanations for dishonesty that go beyond the purely economic imperatives. China is a collectivist society as opposed to the individualist societies of the West. Collectivist societies are low in trust between people who are not family and friends. Strong ingroups operate based on high trust. What appears to Westerners to be dishonest and exploitative behaviour is ethically allowed towards people not in the ingroup. In this case we have expatriate managers coming from a society of high trust towards non-kin expecting objective truth from their partners, but seen by the Chinese as an outgroup. Thus the use of deception is ethically allowable.

Second, the Chinese are pragmatic, meaning that they make the best of any situation. They have not been brought up with the belief in 'truth' as an absolute, and 'untruth' as a sin. Deception for strategic advantage is enshrined in Sunzi's *The Art of War*. By using deception, the Chinese group could pursue their goal of having the foreigners pay.

Third, the members of collectivist societies are very sensitive about having their mistakes publicly noted. Chinese society has been described as 'bonded and entangled' (Worm 1997). Negative information is more damaging to the individuals involved than in a society like most Western societies where ties between individuals are looser. 'Losing face' is more damaging for the Chinese. The settlement in the case study is a typical example of a face-saving solution.

Although in the winery case study there were strong financial imperatives behind the strategy taken by the Chinese side, there were also private needs relating to face and membership of the group. The foreign manager acknowledged this in that he realised winners and losers could not be publicly identified, although everybody knew who they were. Apparently he had had some experience of this when he commented, 'If you do that you have lost face, their authority has been questioned, their leadership has been damaged and they are going to hate you to death.'

Chinese versus foreigners

The Chinese view of their history with the West is of being reduced to semi-colonial status prior to the communist revolution and victory in 1949. As a result there is antagonism, fear and suspicion in regard to foreign business. Coupled with these feelings are the exclusiveness of ingroups in Chinese society and hostility towards outgroups. Individual members of the Chinese side are under pressure to meet the objectives of their side. Anyone who breaks ranks can easily be labelled a 'Hanjian'—a traitor to Chinese interests. It seems far-fetched, but it has reality for the Chinese. Two examples will demonstrate the strength of feeling about what constitutes a 'Chinese traitor'.

A bureaucrat with the Tianjin Economic Development Area told this story to another Chinese person: 'There are a lot of "Chinese traitors". For example, American DOW Chemical negotiated with us. We quoted $380 per square metre. They agreed to that. Some Chinese people said to them, "Two hundred dollars will do. Why pay $380?" In the next negotiation the Americans asked for $200 and it was changed to that. A "Chinese traitor" did this.'

Another case involved a Chinese employee working for a 50–50 joint venture. This account is from the Western finance manager. 'I was working with a young accountant and we needed to finish the work. It was getting late. So we took a taxi to my place, had tea there, and when we'd finished the work he went home by taxi. When he went to get his reimbursement form signed by the Chinese administration manager, she refused. In my naivete I said, "Don't worry. I'll get the American general manager to sign it". He did. Someone let the Chinese administration manager know. The Chinese deputy general manager then put it to the young accountant, "If the Chinese manager disagrees, and doesn't allow you to claim it, you go and ask the American manager, do you?" After that they tried to have the young accountant removed from the joint venture.'

Many Chinese feel unhappy about the way foreign business has performed in the Chinese market. An economic bureaucrat said, 'Normally, the success of one international company makes a lot of Chinese state enterprises get into a disadvantaged competitive situation. Before the Taiwanese fast-noodle group, Dingyi, came to Tianjin, there were seven Chinese fast-noodle factories. Now they have all disappeared.'

And Professor Tang Yunwei, president of the Shanghai University of Finance and Economics, has detailed Chinese concerns about the negative impact of foreign-invested joint ventures on Chinese industry. These concerns are:

1. Foreign products have taken away market share and harmed the reputation of Chinese brands.
2. The preferential treatment given to foreign-invested enterprises has put China's national enterprises into an unfavourable position.
3. Pivotal industries such as automobiles and communications are already monopolised by multinational companies, and chemicals and electronics are increasingly dominated by multinationals.

These developments are in direct contrast to the original intention of admitting foreign firms, which was that they would build the competitiveness of Chinese enterprises in the international market.

In his address, Tang used the words, 'unequal treatment', an echo of the 'unequal treaties' of the nineteenth century, to describe the current privileges extended to foreign invested enterprises as a way of attracting foreign investment. He criticised foreign invested joint ventures because many have side-stepped their responsibility to fund welfare, housing, medical insurance and training. Thus they accept favourable treatment without fulfilling their required social responsibilities (Tang 1995). A Chinese woman in her forties summed up her and her colleagues' feelings when she said, 'We have been slaves to the Westerners'. These are attitudes that may underlie Chinese relationships with foreigners in joint ventures.

III

Foreign managers, Chinese staff

9

Shared management

In the initial phase of foreign investment in China, it was required that foreign companies enter the Chinese market by establishing joint ventures with Chinese enterprises. Wholly-owned enterprises are now permitted, and their popularity equals that of joint ventures. Western companies which entered the Chinese market through the joint venture structure saw virtue in having Chinese partners as an entry mechanism into the local market and as go-betweens with the bureaucracy. They also used joint venturing with huge Chinese enterprises as a way of dominating the market against the threat of other multinationals and local companies in the same industry. As part of the joint venture structure the Chinese want to share management equally, regardless of their equity level. However, shared management is a potential time bomb.

Shared management joint ventures, no matter what the nationality of the joint venture partners, or where they are located globally, face the divisive forces of two partners involved in a struggle for power. Managers are appointed by their own side, and generally see their future as lying with their own side, so naturally they attempt to implement the agenda of their parent organisation. This conclusion comes from a study of the issues of joint venture management carried out by J. Peter

Killing. In his remarkably insightful little book *Strategies for Joint Venture Success* (1983) he writes that 50 per cent of the 74 shared management ventures he examined were liquidated or reorganised due to poor performance, as against 15 per cent where there was a dominant parent and management was not shared.

When Chinese–foreign joint ventures were established, Chinese managers dispatched to them from the Chinese parent believed that foreign participation would be short term. Once the capital, technology and advanced management skills had been acquired, the Chinese would proceed alone without need for foreign participation. A Chinese manager at the Volkswagen Shanghai factory said, 'We had the idea that everything would be better in a joint venture.

'Western management know-how could be easily learned overnight, and advanced technology could be applied at once . . . In the past 30 years, the Chinese have repeatedly been told that they are their country's masters, the owners of enterprises and in a position to have the final say. At a joint venture where they own 50 per cent, they no longer have that position . . . intentional attempts to obstruct the scheme of co-operation have been known.' (Hoon-Halbauer 1996, pp. 140–1)

This manager highlights that Chinese people want to be their own masters and this can lead to subversion of the Western manager's schemes.

As for the quality of the person chosen to run the joint venture and deal with the joint venture board of directors, Killing concluded: 'This is no place for a rookie.' The following case study demonstrates how true this can be in the case of Chinese–foreign joint ventures.

Case study: 'They lost a bit of face'

The manager in this case study was the first general manager of his company's joint venture manufacturing plant in Shanghai. The joint venture was based on a former state enterprise. The plant was rundown and worker morale was low. Although the Western manager didn't know it when he began, the market was highly competitive and was to become increasingly so during his three years in China.

The Western company had been told that once they had improved the product it would sell, as the general manager said, 'like hot cakes'. In fact, quality rapidly improved, but selling the product turned out to be a difficult task. The Chinese side had expected that the foreign partner would do well automatically. So both sides had expectations that were impossible to meet. Here the manager discusses his three years spent setting up the joint venture.

'We knew it wasn't going to be easy. We went in open-minded, ready to learn. Our senior Chinese managers had their own barrows to push, their own liaisons, their own loyalties to other people, no matter how much they profess that their loyalty is to the company. The husband worked for us, their wives for a state enterprise. Nothing was confidential. The Chinese in this particular period have come out of a violent period where they were selling out their soul. In a city like Shanghai, everyone is out to survive. So I'm not too cynical.'

Conflict

'On the joint venture board at least two people were executives in the previous Chinese company. We were doing things a lot better in many areas for which they formerly had responsibility, so they lost a bit of face over that. They would attack at board meetings—they'd attack me and my performance. They were actually attacking people who worked for me. They were petty little issues. It would go on for two or three hours. I was advised to soak in the blows and enjoy it! I used to get advance notice. It was destructive and distracted from what we were trying to do.

'They had axes to grind. In one particular person it was loss of face. I wouldn't be surprised if there were other agendas. The state wanted returns as quickly as possible, before we had established the business and sales. I think they thought that we would come in with huge amounts of money to splash around, huge amounts of technology, and we'd make money, so they wouldn't have to make efficiencies. We were sparse with our money—we targeted it carefully. We didn't go in with new technology. We thought they had good equipment and we wanted to make it work the way it was meant to work.'

Upgrading the technology always involved the general manager in a boardroom battle because the Chinese directors wanted to buy local plant and thus keep the money in local Chinese factories. Although he would have preferred to buy locally, he couldn't find local equipment suited to a modern plant. The Chinese were suspicious of his motives in buying offshore equipment and fought it strongly.

Response

Of his management experiences he said, "There were challenges coming from every direction. I just tried to slow down, to have a sense of humour, just enjoy it, try to keep the original goals in view, try to be honest with everyone. We should have that honesty to fall back on, let our message get across to people. We were desperate to keep the operation going with the right sort of price.

'We went to China because it was a chance to create something. Further down the track it will be part of a huge new organisation. We had resilience in surviving what was thrown at us. It was described to us as a "hostile environment". I thought that was over the top. But it really is hostile. Just the actual environment itself: the people, the language, the foreignness, people looking at you as a foreigner—you want to scream, "Stop looking at me!". Your senses get overloaded. It's just so different! And you are also there to do a job, and are expected to do it to the same standard as in our home office. The hostility from the Chinese side was so bad at times that I got the finance manager to make sure that whatever happened we had a few thousand dollars in the bank to pay for our airfares out and a few bottles of champagne to drink on the way to the airport . . . '

The company didn't continue with the joint venture. Over the three years the Chinese partner's real agenda emerged and it was too different from the foreign company's. The Chinese wanted quick returns and management control. The foreign side tired of Chinese interference in the running of the business. They were restrained by the Chinese deputy managers in sales, marketing, finance and production. Since the foreign partner was putting in all the money, they decided to buy out the Chinese partner and gain full control.

Comment

Unexpected management problems

This general manager was experienced, in his mid-forties and successful in his home environment. But he was faced with the problems of joint ventures in China at this particular time in history: expectations on both sides that were unrealistic, senior Chinese managers who saw their past prestige and power being undermined, and different agendas on both sides.

Chinese managers expected foreign companies to invest large amounts of money that would save state-owned enterprises from the heavy debt burden most carried. Foreign funds would allow them to maintain their enterprises intact—in particular, to maintain high staffing levels and social welfare support. Nothing would change except that the foreign exchange and technology would flood in and profits would rise. Chinese managers were directed to carry out the government policy of 'localisation'—that is, to give maximum opportunity to local industry to supply foreign invested enterprises. This was directed at preserving foreign exchange.

In this joint venture the Chinese managers also wanted to retain their control over marketing. Their parent company had its own distribution system which worked on high volume, small margins and no brand awareness. The driving mentality was, 'Just get it out the gate.' The foreign manager, on the other hand, had come with the expectation that foreign business methods would be adopted. These included world best practice in production, which implied a substantial reduction in the workforce, marketing based on brands, building market share and reinvesting profits into the business.

The Western manager ran headlong into conflict on the board and with his senior managers. The irreconcilable agendas were expressed through divided loyalties among staff, suspicion and distrust. The foreign company's circumspection about investing large amounts of

foreign exchange was a source of dispute. This was followed by the reality of market indifference to the new
brands. Chinese people just didn't want to pay for a
foreign product when adequate and cheap local products
were available. This led to poor financial outcomes,
resulting in recriminations from Chinese board members.
They saw it as a betrayal of their trust in the foreign
company's ability to make profits.

The Western manager's method of dealing with these
multiple difficulties and hostility was to 'slow down',
'have a sense of humour', 'try to keep the original goals
in view' and 'try to be honest with everyone'. Having a
sense of humour is relevant in China, because so many
things happen that don't appear to conform to Western
logic and over which a foreigner has little or no control.
They are produced from conditions not known to Westerners, or obey rules that are unfamiliar. The result for
a Western manager can be high levels of stress and
frustration.

This general manager gave an example of the unpredictable nature of management problems. In the streets
outside the factory, local people would set up a marketplace. Their stalls spread out over the whole street so
that the transport trucks couldn't get through to the
factory or out again. The manager tried to have the
market relocated, and the Public Security Bureau assisted
him in this. But unfortunately the locals preferred this
location, and several times a week they would return to
disrupt deliveries to and dispatches from the factory.
Sometimes local residents would stage a sit-in outside the
factory gates, so-called revolutionary action, to protest
about noise or traffic or some other issue related to the
factory. The sit-in was invariably to demand monetary
compensation for the local residents.

The influence of the bottom line

Chinese partner concern with matters on their own side,
to the exclusion of the Western partner's interests, is a

commonly reported joint venture experience for Western managers. At this joint venture as financial results failed to improve, Chinese criticism of the general manager increased. Killing (1983) wrote of shared joint venture management: 'You can paper over the cracks and divided loyalties in the good times, it's in the hard times that the differences in underlying allegiances really show up.' This has been the experience of many Western companies in China as profits have failed to materialise. Difficulties relating to financial matters led to secretiveness on the Chinese side.

A good example of the secretive behaviour that Chinese partners adopt was reported by the expatriate general manager of another joint venture. Chinese members of the board of the joint venture met and declared a dividend without informing him. When he found out and asked why he had not been invited to the meeting, the Chinese directors replied, 'Because you would have voted against it'. The company was in debt. When he questioned how a decision had been made in his absence when the articles stated that all decisions had to be unanimous, they replied: 'Oh, it doesn't matter. This is China.'

The Chinese directors had made promises of a dividend to the local government and the Party. That the company had serious debt was secondary to the pressures on the Chinese side to appear profitable by distributing a dividend. Again and again, foreign general managers have reported that a serious conflict arises at board level over the policy on residuals; whether they are to be distributed as dividends, invested in other businesses run by the Chinese board members, or reinvested in the business for its long-term growth as the foreign manager expects. Chinese directors are usually linked with other enterprises and the local bureaucracy, and thus respond to these pressures and not just to the interests of the joint venture business. They are networked into their parent enterprise, and their future depends upon being able to meet parent demands. This is understandable when it is considered that both the Chinese parent enterprise and its affiliated government bureaus face the pressing social problems of overemployment, unemployment and fiscal distress. The individuals themselves are also participants in the 'get rich is glorious' movement whose credo is private gain. In contrast, most Western managers focus on the long-term business objectives of building the business and expanding market share.

If a business is not doing well financially, it undermines the authority of all expatriate managers. An expatriate manager, contemplating his difficulty in changing the attitude of workers, said, 'I don't think they were told how badly off this factory was. When we bought it it was 35 million RMB in debt. But no one told them. No one said, "This factory is going to shut down". The workers always say that when it was state-owned it was running well. When we come in and say, "We haven't made budget this month, we are losing money for the expenses we have", they think it is our problem. So anything bad that happens now is because of us.'

Although the manager in the case study largely enjoyed his work, he admitted that he had had some down times in China. 'The thing that has brought down times has been relationships where I've felt that I am getting nowhere. Being excluded, being treated as a foreign devil and that we are here to exploit rather than to help—the attitude that we have been ripped off for centuries by the foreign devils, so it is our turn to rip off the foreign devils.'

10

Culture change

One of the major challenges for an expatriate manager is introducing Western workplace culture. This has been necessary because of the workplace culture inherited from the state-run enterprises of the communist period. Staff trained in that organisational culture were used to management by Communist Party cadres, rather than by professional business managers. These had been successively displaced during the 1950s. State-run enterprises were marked by poor work practices, unsystematic production systems, backward technology and a reward system unrelated to performance. They produced to quotas, and inputs and outputs were determined by a central plan. Once the quota was reached, employees had nothing more to do. Because under-employed workers were retained by the enterprise, it was quite common for workers to have only three days' work out of six. Reports from Western business people who went into these factories in the 1970s noted the malaise that affected them. One manager said, 'In factory after factory they would say 1000 were employed, but you'd only see about 200 people actually working'. Purchasing and sales people spent time having cups of tea in relevant work units to keep up the relationships needed to secure supplies and assist sales. The concept of actively building market share was not one of their concerns.

The state enterprises had financial structures that had nothing to do with market forces. They were owned by government bureaus, and each enterprise's taxes were contracted by negotiation with its bureau. In general, an enterprise would pay the standard tax on a fixed level of profit whether they met the profit level or not, and they usually paid nothing on any profits above the agreed level. The bureau then negotiated revenue-sharing with higher levels of government. When enterprises could not meet their expenses, the government provided loss subsidies (Wong et al. 1995).

With technical and management skill levels lower than Western managers expected, even among university graduates, accomplishing change has not been as straightforward as head office planners assumed. This has meant a much slower progress towards world best practice, products that are more expensive and of lesser quality than the multinational's other global products, and the need for a longer time-frame to address these problems. When possible, a strategy has been for companies to recruit young staff untainted by the old communist culture. Expatriate staff charged with effecting culture change have a hard task when, as in the next case study, the ratio of expatriates to local staff is in the vicinity of 3:350.

Case study: 'The foreigners are no good—listen to *us*'

This case study is told from the point of view of two young expatriate production managers. They work for a large multinational with huge financial resources. However, this apparent advantage counts for little in their day-to-day struggles to gain control over the Chinese workers in their joint venture factory. The factory makes moulds for glass bottles and containers.

'This joint venture is a 70–30 partnership. The Chinese ripped off our parent company right from the start. The Chinese were supposed to supply the plant we were in, but when it came to the time our company had to supply the plant. Our company has been here four years and we have gone through four Chinese deputy general managers. One of them ripped off our company regarding the housing fund. He organised to build five houses, and he built six houses—one for himself. That caused a riot among the workers. So there has been a lot of corruption.

'It is hard for them to realise that they no longer have lifetime employment, lifetime security. Other problem areas are quality issues, productivity issues, our customers' demands about delivery, simple market forces. The customers ask for certain things in their drawings, but the Chinese managers say, "They don't need that. We're not going to do that". They haven't had to do it in the past, so they think they don't need to do it now. We will pull them up and say, "That size is no good". They reply, "We've never checked it in the past; it doesn't need to be done". It's very hard for them to break the mould of the past, of the last 30 years.'

Reorganisaton

One of their first actions was to move a lot of senior Chinese managers into non-critical areas. They felt this was necessary because they observed that the shop floor felt intimidated by the older-style, senior Chinese management.

'The former Chinese production manager could say to the workers, "You do this", "You do that". He had control over the workers. They were petrified of him. If we were talking to someone with our interpreter and he walked around the corner, they'd shut up and pretend they were working and that we were just looking over their shoulder. When you see things like that you know that he put pressure on them: "What were you saying?". He was a blockage to the extent that he thought he was the only one who knew anything.'

The two expatriate operations managers felt that by removing the hierarchy they could have more control over the workers and that would make a difference to the production issues. However, because the Chinese managers feel they have lost their authority and status, it has created friction between the senior level of Chinese management and the expatriates.

The shift managers are now given more responsibility, as happens in the West. The operations manager would usually delegate jobs to the shift managers and they have to organise everything. The results of this reorganisation have been mixed. Some shift managers are proving to be very good at what they are doing, while some others are finding it difficult. They are afraid of making the decisions. They have never had that responsibility in the past because the operations manager made all the decisions and disciplined the workers.

'The shift managers used to come in all the time saying, "This person is no good, this person is no good". Now we say to them, "OK. We'll make a scene of it, but we are going to involve you. We are going to say to the worker, 'Shift Manager Liu said you did this wrong'". The shift managers now have to think they cannot just run into us and say, "He's no good, he made a mistake". Because if we take it further, which they always want us to do, we are going to be saying,

"Shift Manager Liu said this, and that is why I am disciplining you".

'Things get hot in meetings where they tell white lies. The lies are stupid. They are just out of the blue. They have no meaning for the subject whatsoever. You say to the manager, "Why didn't those parts go out?" And he blames it on something that had no relevance whatsoever. So you ask another question, and by the fourth question you are getting closer to the real reason. By then you are starting to get frustrated. "We have been down this line before. This is the third time this has happened. Do I have to give you a written warning?" And then one of the Chinese deputy general managers gets involved and says, "We don't need to do that".'

Getting tough

'We say the Chinese have to learn, but we are having to learn so much ourselves. What is difficult for us is that things which take a minute or five minutes at home take an hour or two days here. We get frustrated. If we see someone doing something wrong, we go straight to the shift manager and ask him, "What are you doing about it?" When we started we were too open-ended, too trusting. At home we would leave instructions for the shift managers over the weckend. We'd pretty much enjoy ourselves on the weekend—watch TV, go to the football—and know that the jobs would be done. Here we two operations managers are on shift duty. We cover 20 of the 24 hours. Head office wants only one expatriate to be responsible for production. In a Western system we don't have two people with the same responsibilities. Simon and I say, "No, the problems are big. We need two people to fix them".

'Last weekend the set work wasn't done. So we said, "OK, no one gets any overtime payments". I think they are starting to realise that we are starting to cotton on to what they are doing. They are very good at blaming someone else, and playing with us because we don't know everything that is going on and cannot know everything. They blame the machines. We have the worst machines in the world! We have started to say, "That's your responsibility. You've got to make sure the machine doesn't do that". He says, "But it is hard, it is hard". We say, "You are a manager and get paid accordingly. Start doing it". As the pressure goes on, some are standing up very high, and some unfortunately are not.

'We've made operators work in their free time on jobs that haven't been done properly. Previously they would lose their bonus or they'd be sent home for three months to think about it, but we'd have to pay them their basic salary. Now we say, "No, you stay here and fix it". So people have had to come in on Saturday to fix a job.

'We just had to dismiss one guy because he was stealing. It was one of the new guys, our most outstanding employee. He had just come back from a training course with the highest marks. Simon and I were really down for two days. Why? He was one of our good boys. He would really think about a problem. Instead of just coming in and saying, "I have this problem", he'd think about it, fix it, and come and tell us what he had done. It is very rare to find people who will make decisions for themselves. He stole the keyboard off the computer. He took it out on a particular shift. We knew what shift and we said that if it didn't come back the whole shift would be punished. The peer pressure. They must have known who took it. It came back and we knew who took it.

'There is a resentment between the old and new shift managers. No one likes the people we employed after the joint venture was formed, because they earn more money. All the old people have power. The shift managers never tell you when an older employee has done something wrong. They will only tell you when a new person has. There is one shift manager whose shift isn't that bad because he knows what he is doing. He has been here over 30 years. He certainly knows how to do his job, but they say he is on the corrupt side to the extent that when he disagrees with the things that we want to do, he'll say to the workers, "that won't work".

'When the company first came in, it tried to throw money at the existing employees thinking it would motivate them. It didn't work. Now they are highly paid and they still have no motivation. If you were to take the money off them now, they would be very unhappy and totally against us.

'They are slowly getting the message and are starting to be concerned to the extent that we have lost four key staff in the last month. That is how they show their concern: they go and find another job. Part of that you could blame us for, because we told them that it's not in a bright situation and that we must improve or else the place may fold. Instead of digging their heels in and saying, "Well, I'm going to work hard to turn the place around", they say, "Well, I'd better find another job now".

'When it was a state-owned company, if they made two moulds a day it was pretty good. Now they make eight. They think they've done much better than ever before, but really world best practice would mean fifteen. It is very hard for them to think, "I've got to hit fifteen". They are happy in what they are doing because it is so much better than what they are used to.

'They accept scrap and rework. The scrap rates are very high. They have an unusual consumer attitude. If they go to a shop and buy five things—for example, CDs—they expect that two of the products won't work, so they buy two CDs not to work. They have the same attitude here. They make so many products expecting to scrap a certain amount. But that might be three months' salary they have scrapped. There is a lot of money involved.

'A big part of the problem is our parent company's investment philosophy. The equipment is too sophisticated for them. They went from a bicycle to a Rolls-Royce overnight. There wasn't an intermediate level where they built their skills and their technology. They've been dumped in with the highest technology in the world and told, "Now compete at world best practice". In all areas of business we are still 30–50 per cent down. We use the same materials, same machinery, same tooling—the difference is the person behind the machine. We don't blame the person. We blame the system.'

Local–foreign conflict

'Our partner is the local Light Industry Bureau. They are more interested in our social welfare than in getting the plant operational. We have had a lot of problems with the Light Industry Bureau in the sense that they see the expatriates as a very expensive item, and they feel that they can do the job themselves without the expats. The Chinese partner at this plant has too much to say. The personnel department reports to the Chinese deputy general manager and not the expatriate general manager. Although we control the technology and the process, they still have control over people.'

The company sells to joint venture packaging companies. However, the market hasn't expanded according to expectations. The company's moulds are 30 per cent more expensive than the Chinese mould shops' and a lot better quality. The problem is that most Chinese products do not warrant high quality, so local companies buy the cheap ones. It is only the big manufacturers who try and export who want the company's moulds. But even the big companies, if they are making for locals, buy the local Chinese moulds. This economic issue has a bad impact on the two expatriate managers.

'It has been difficult for us to get the runs on the board. We came to help them improve the business to the extent that they sit back and say, "Wow! These guys really know what they are doing". We came to increase productivity, increase quality. We have a feeling that things are going better now than they used to, but it doesn't show in the figures. Last month we had a good rate. But it had been achieved once or twice before. Until the people start saying, "Things are changing and it is going better . . . ". Sales at the moment are low and slow. We are trying to increase productivity, and the best way is to have more orders flowing all the time. But we stop and we start.

'We are getting the blame. We've had some of the Chinese hierarchy come down to get us to change some of our ways, and do some things differently. And that is one of the big problems, the Westerners against the Chinese. We are all management, but sometimes we sit down at a table and all the foreigners sit on one side and all the Chinese on the other. We argue over things like two opposing teams. We really should be together as a single management base. It makes it hard. I think the Chinese deputy general managers are saying to the Chinese staff, "The foreigners are no good—listen to *us*".

'We have a training course planned regarding trust. Trust is a big issue. They don't trust us. They see us as being temporary employees here, earning a lot of money. We might come in and make a racket and stir them up and then we are gone, and they are left to pick up the pieces. They unfortunately don't see that we are here to help. They think that we are here to cause them trouble and grief, and to feather our own nest. It is public knowledge how much the expats cost the organisation. Our living standards are high in comparison with theirs.

'The language barrier is difficult because we cannot thrash over something. And that is where we think that our interpreters are instructed by the Chinese side. There are many things that go on in here that are for Chinese ears only. There are many times when the interpreters would like to tell us things, but they know that we are only here for two years. They are under pressure from their side. If we hear something, we take action immediately. And their side knows where the information came from. I wouldn't want to have the interpreter's job. When things finally happen we tell the interpreter off because he didn't tell us straightaway. I think the Chinese do more than that. Especially some of the managers. A lot is for Chinese ears only.

'There's a board of directors with our expatriate general manager and a Chinese deputy general manager and two representatives from the Light Industry Bureau. Last Wednesday the Chinese went in and said that the two expats, Simon and myself, were useless and they have cost us business. We hadn't been able to meet deliveries. They named jobs and facts. The very next day they shook our hands and thanked us for getting the productivity up . . . That part has been the most difficult for me, to be able to look them in the eye. We are a lot more up-front. We don't understand that way the Chinese do things. They are always very nice to your face, but behind your back they say whatever they want.

'Our company headquarters are aware of things like this, but it makes our work so hard. They say, "They always do that. Don't be too concerned". We are concerned in that it rubs off on the people. They will say things from the board meetings to the operators: "It's the foreigners' ideas that make us go wrong".

'We are the easiest people to blame, for the reasons that we can't understand what they are saying for one, and we earn so much money in comparison. It boils them up sometimes. We are in a non-negotiable stage at the moment. We haven't any proof apart from our own feelings, but we are starting to show better results. But until we can get into a sustained position they will continue to bicker. We are losing over 10 million RMB a year.

'Being in a joint venture is the biggest problem. It is going to be better to buy out our partner. Then we can say, "You, you, you, you and you—

you're gone. We don't want you any more". We can do it our way. In a wholly-owned enterprise if the operator has a bad attitude, out the door! Here you have to go up and see Chairman Wong, the trade union Party official, who's then got to go and see the Light Industry Bureau. At the end of it you might be able to get rid of them, yes, but you have to pay them 20 000 RMB, and then they are going to donate it back to the Party who then go and find them another job. They know that they are still "lifers" here.'

According to the two operations managers, 'The only advantage of having a Chinese joint venture partner is that they handle relations with the local government. There is a budget for taking Chinese officials for dinner twice a month. It is usually at Chairman Mao's favourite duck restaurant. We've been a few times. We don't like it.'

Comment

Here are two young managers effectively out of control. They have no respect from the local Chinese and are without the maturity to put their stamp of authority on the situation. There is no doubt that they have been placed in a difficult situation because their company did not know enough about China before they made the investment. Even now they struggle with ignorance in their own head office. In fact, the CEO of their company, when its eight joint ventures in China were announced, was reported in the press as saying: 'If some of them fall over, so be it!'

In the previous chapter we saw the conflicts at board level between Chinese and Westerners. In this chapter we have seen the same conflict on the shop floor. What has happened to these two managers has been the experience in many joint ventures—due to the characteristics of the Chinese market, sales have not improved significantly for the joint venture. As a result, the Chinese partners are dissatisfied and the expatriate managers haven't been able to build credibility. The Chinese therefore start to question the usefulness of Western management and the cost of expatriates. To avoid this problem, some companies have disguised the expatriate cost factor. The Western side has a negative opinion of the Chinese due to their early experience of the Chinese partners not fulfilling their initial undertaking to build the plant and of corrupt practices on the part of senior management.

Culture change

This has been made extremely difficult, if not impossible, by management conflict and the continuing presence of the former Chinese managers. The two expatriate managers have undertaken radical structural change by removing the senior Chinese managers from their former positions and pushing responsibility down to middle management level. With the former Chinese managers still on site, it is likely that the workers, including the shift managers, are still locked into the Chinese power networks and bound by loyalty and pre-existing personal ties.

The move to give responsibility to the shift managers is not well thought through. It is based on an individualistic culture. Chinese culture is group-centred. The Chinese boss usually dominates the power structure, just as the former operations manager did. The staff depend on the boss for directions, definition of problems and decision-making about the best solutions. Middle management does not have these powers as they do in most Western companies. In bringing about such a radical change the Western manager needs to act as a coach. 'Acting as a coach, anticipate problems on the job they will face, then walk them through the problems and rehearse effective ways of solving them . . . step-by-step anticipate things that will bother them and help them deal with those issues.' (Fallon 1997) By this method, middle managers are shielded from failure and exposure to public criticism.

The foreign managers see attending to the task as the main issue. They do not understand that for the Chinese managers interpersonal issues may be the main issues. The situation in which Chinese shift managers have been placed to combine decision-making responsibility with the power of disciplining subordinates may bring with it problems in the interpersonal area that are unanticipated and not understood by the expatriates.

Traditional leadership has been premised on age and seniority. It is obvious that there will be major problems associated with disenfranchising senior management and replacing it with young people in a context where the people issues are still controlled by the Chinese partner.

White lies

Indirectness is the natural communication style of the Chinese because they belong to the group of cultures that are 'high context'. Most Chinese are cautious about voicing negative information or information that would cause them to lose face. It is arguable that because of their childhood upbringing most Chinese derive their self-esteem from peer approval to a greater extent than in English-speaking cultures. Facts with negative implications for their own status within their group are suppressed.

In relations with foreigners, Chinese face is in an insecure environment. Foreigners, not understanding the rules of face and the harm that can be done by public disclosure, cannot be relied upon to exercise discretion. Chinese conclude that in relations with Westerners the safest route is to dissimulate, to hide damaging information. A Western manager described Chinese relationships as 'sticky' (Harris 1997). He meant that most business decision-making in China has to take into account the relationships between people. Employees may be relatives, or they may be in a wide network of relationships going back decades. There are many ramifications for Chinese employees. A practical one may be that since housing is a valuable part of the total employment package, losing it due to problems at work throws a whole family out of their accommodation.

In a public situation such as in this case study where shift managers are put on the spot about problems, the Chinese avoid open conflict and loss of face by using a pragmatic strategy—white lies. Strategies that may circumvent the use of white lies include: building trust, not putting people 'on the spot', using the group rather than the individual (as in a focus group, where one person puts forward the deliberations of the group), keeping calm, and using individual interviews and indirect communication (Fallon 1997).

Chinese staff views

There are dangers in using a style of supervision that is based on democratic Western models. That has already been established in this case study. A young Chinese manager in the factory made some observations about the old workforce and the foreign managers.

'The foreign managers asked us to lift the production levels. But nothing improved because staff were still doing it according to the old ways and there was no punishment. The foreigners knew there was chaos. They don't want to do anything about it. They come in the morning and just sit in their offices for a long time. They don't normally walk through the plant. I think this is because Western people believe in self-reliance. They don't know about Chinese laziness and slave characteristics. They probably cannot feel psychologically comfortable if they are too hard on us. They are too kind and too nice and there is too much democracy. The expatriate general manager has a suggestion box; anyone can report anything to him. But what is reported may not be right. The foreigners can't speak the language, so they can't talk to us directly. A lot of problems come from a lack of management strength.

'There is a lot of stealing. The guards just sleep in their work time. Whoever wants to come into the plant compound can come in. The regulation says bikes cannot go into the plant. Everyone rides in. Families and relatives come in to have a shower, just like in a state-owned company, not like in a foreign company at all. People are not allowed to chat and visit other workers when they work. But when you go into the offices everyone is in groups chatting away. If you have a good relationship with the shift manager you can get overtime work on the weekends for a lot better pay. That is to do with the master–apprentice relationship from the past. When the shift managers give overtime to certain workers there is a commission in it for the shift manager. The middle managers block all information to the foreigners. The foreigners don't understand this. The interpreter does not translate everything for them. If you have a good relationship with him he might translate more. So the foreigners know very little about the facts of the situation.

'When a new young foreign technical expert arrived, the workers put up a big character poster saying, "Go back home foreign expert". Some workers have been working for twenty or more years in this plant. They know quite a lot in some areas. The foreign expert cannot know everything. The workers say he makes so much money and controls us, but he is no better than us. Sometimes his directives don't work. The workers say, "What kind of expert is he? When I started working in this factory he was just learning to walk". They look down on him. If they don't want to work, they won't work.'

This Chinese manager had worked in a Taiwanese–Chinese joint venture company and found there that staff were controlled strictly by salary penalties and a 'three strikes and you're out' disciplinary policy. The section managers rated the performance of each worker on quality and quantity and assigned a score. This score formed the basis for the bonus distribution. Naturally the system gave a lot of power to the section managers, but, she concluded, 'That is how Asian people manage Asian people'. It also is a policy learned by many Western managers. Her report on what is going on among Chinese workers in the Western–Chinese joint venture not only makes clear the management difficulties in a formerly state-owned enterprise, but illustrates the problem of small numbers of expatriates managing a large Chinese workforce. It also illustrates what the executive in Chapter 8 said about the danger of sending young and inexperienced managers to China: 'If you send a twenty-year old, unless he is exceptional he is going to go head-on there, and he's going to be exploited, abused and used.'

11

Skills differential

It is hard to find highly skilled workers and managers in China. Only 1.1 per cent of the population over 25 years of age has post-secondary education. Of the current college-aged student cohort, China has only 191 students per 100 000 in post-secondary education. In comparison the United States has 5653, Canada 7197, Australia 3178, Germany 3051 and the UK 2406 per 100 000.

'Train, train, train' is the motto of most companies in China that are serious about quality production and the future localisation of management staff. Some very large companies have set up their own universities and training institutes. Coming to terms with the reality of this lack of skilled staff is a learning experience for foreign managers. The next case study demonstrates some ordinary problems that occur because of low skill levels and unfamiliarity with Chinese thinking about tasks they are assigned. It is obvious that expatriate guidance and control is necessary at this stage in China's technological development.

Case study: 'I could not imagine such a thing happening'

This manager is in a 50–50 joint venture. He exercises close management supervision because of the low level of technical knowledge and hidden agendas on the Chinese side. He came up against these problems at the very beginning of the joint venture.

'We installed a plant on the analysis of water, and we found out later that the water they sent to the labs to be analysed was in fact mineral water they bought in the supermarket, not the water coming from the tap.

'My mistake was that I couldn't imagine such a thing happening. I trusted the person I asked to test the water, to take a water sample from the local supply and give it to me and we would send it to the lab. Whether he went to the tap and it was that part of the day when the water was really brown and he was ashamed of it, or he thought, "This is going to be analysed, the quality of the water is going to be known, and I know the person who is running the purification plant, and he is going to be in deep trouble".

'You can bring in all sorts of theories. But on the day it wasn't the right water. It wasn't analysed correctly. I took a technical decision based on that. What I should have done was go with him, hold his hand and look at the water falling into the bottle. So this is one thing: check everything as much as you can.'

To achieve this close checking he has established a parallel structure. One person does the work, the other checks. This way he addresses the problems of trust, of training and of staff turnover. If one leaves, there is someone else there who knows what has been happening. The checkers are people with status, expatriates. They may be Chinese, but they have the status of expatriates. If they want to keep their salary package they have to do the job. The foreign partner thus has control over them, which is not the case with all the other Chinese employees.

He wanted to develop responsibility in employees to improve their handling of the job and their self-esteem, but this didn't work out for an unexpected reason. 'We wanted them to put a dose of chemical into the product. We said, "We'll give you the dose, 1 gram per litre, and you just work out how much that is for the amount of litres in the tanks, add it to the product, and you will be fine".

'The weakness was that I didn't check if they were able to implement that. They didn't know how to calculate how many kilos for the tank. I should have said, "We are going to operate this way. I will give you a dose. You have two tanks, so you tell me exactly how many kilos you calculate are needed and report it to me". If you do it this way they will know that you have been strong and checked everything. This way, if the person you delegate to is incapable of doing the job, he could say, "I don't really like doing that job. I know someone who is keen to replace me. I want to concentrate on another area". He won't say he doesn't know how to make the calculation.

'That person was put sideways. In China you have a lot of people in office positions. They are given a chance, and they're not able to do it, and you can't fire them really, so they are under-used. They've got a little office somewhere—they do nothing, but they are still there. In the cities you spend your time training people, and when the person is trained, you have basically built a little chief. They have millions of little leaders who don't want to do anything. When you have power in China you have access to a lot of other people for part of your wages. So you are buying free time.'

Character of the expatriates

'In our production we need Westerners or Chinese we trust, who have a permanency in the mind, who are going to do the production work, keep training people, and be the guarantee that the managers are working when you are not there. Because when you leave, they get someone else to do the work. Because of that you have quality problems. There is a huge turnover of people. And you've got to keep at it much more than in the West. In China it can change a lot from one month to the next. You have to be very worried about that.

'You must make sure that the general manager is not seen as someone who is dictatorial, who gives instructions and says, "You do this because I told you so". The best way to present things is to say, "Well, that's the way it is done in my country. We are making the best product in the world and that is the way we do it". You never say, "Your orders are to do it like this, and if you don't do it like this then . . . ". They won't do it.

'If they hate you, they will not let you know what they are feeling, but you will feel it very quickly nevertheless. You always have to scrub the surface because you've got to look for signals, and rhythm, to find out if the relationship is working or not. If you suspect there is a problem, you are not going to learn anything by going to the person and saying, "Have I done anything wrong? Perhaps I have made a mistake and didn't realise. Can we sort this out?" If you do that it will probably make it worse, because you are bending forwards for the person and they would not see that as a matter of strength. That would be another reason for them not to respect you. You have to make them understand that you are not going to do anything silly to them, but that they have things to lose by not co-operating. If by being a diplomat you show too much patience and weakness, you are never going to get an outcome.'

Comment

Lack of discipline

This manager, like all foreign managers, is learning about Chinese staff as he goes along. It is impossible for him as a foreigner to predict Chinese behaviour, or to understand the motivations of the Chinese staff. His response is pragmatic: not to delve into the relationships and agendas, but to employ expatriates or Chinese with experience overseas to check the work. Because each has individual accountability with financial rewards and penalties, there is quality control over the work they do. In their home company the ratio of managers to workers is 1:8. In China, at least for the present, they require it to be 1:3. Many foreign managers complain of their Chinese staff, 'You tell them one thing, and they do another', or 'You can tell them something until you are blue in the face but it won't make a blind bit of difference'.

The kind of thing that causes Western managers to express their feelings so forcefully is illustrated in this story from a joint venture factory. Staff were told not to use personal computer disks and programs in the plant's computers. The reason was that there are many viruses in China that are not controllable by Western security systems. If any of these viruses got into the plant's computer-based production system it would wreak havoc. Although there was a complete prohibition on personal computer disks, staff disobeying the ban have brought the whole plant to a standstill a number of times. The plant had to shut for weeks each time.

Another observation made by Western managers related to this undisciplined approach is that staff don't arrive at work at the assigned time, but wander in anything up to two hours late. These behaviours require strict supervision.

Low skill levels

Most difficulties in changing the culture of organisations in China can be attributed to the low skill levels of staff and their total lack of experience of Western quality and Western systems. Staff have not had experience with the high-technology machinery installed in foreign factories. They have no experience of the quality common in the West. They have not worked with the systems and analytical management techniques of Western business.

So when a Western manager gives directions, the expectation in the minds of the Chinese may be entirely different from what is in the manager's mind. A Western technician installing air-conditioning in a new factory made a study of local Chinese air-conditioning systems in the restaurants he visited. This gave him a better understanding of where his workmen were coming from, of what their standards were. His on-the-ground research uncovered the following: 'The grill into the room is meant to get 80 litres per second of air. The system might be doing mach 2 but nothing is coming into the big room. So the restaurant staff just open the door. The pipes are full of dirt and rubble. When they start up the air-conditioning system you can hear this awful clunk as something flies into the impeller on the pumps. We go to a lot of trouble to tape up the ends of the pipes so that no dirt or dust or stones or rubble go down inside the pipes. They don't bother to do that.'

On his own job, even though he walked around all the time and supervised the 40 Chinese workers very closely, he still found it difficult to monitor their work. 'We had some dampers fitted in between the ducts. We didn't find out till later that the ducts wouldn't open because they had twisted it a little bit. We had a lot of rework to do. When I was experienced, I spent most of my time concentrating on catching the faults before they became disasters. They just don't understand that the equipment costs so much.'

They don't understand why things must be done a certain way. When he took out his special test equipment worth over US$20 000, they said to him, 'We don't need that'. He felt like saying to them, 'That's why we're here'. He is a kind person and he kept his mouth shut. Of course, there are members of the Chinese government who know the importance of Western technology and quality systems. That is why they insist that major construction contracts have foreign partners to bring quality to the building.

A construction company had trouble getting contract workers to build a surrounding wall to the quality required. The workers were used to the rough brick walls that surround Chinese compounds. Since this was a building to the best international standards, the construction manager required the same quality for the wall. He said, 'We just wanted to make sure the fence wouldn't fall over, that it was straight. We would say, "That's not good enough. Pull it down and do it again". We got through four different contractors. We were getting a name for being awkward to work with, difficult to do a job with, wanting impossible quality. What we did in the end was we brought in an Australian to work in gumboots and with the shovel to show them how to pour concrete. Once we did that, the actual workers on site were very keen to do it properly. They didn't have the skills. But once they were shown the skills, they became very good workers. It changed the whole scene around.'

Western managers often find that Chinese staff devise the 'wrong solution' to problems when they are actually thinking they are being self-reliant. The 'wrong solutions' are usually because the Chinese simply haven't had the experience of advanced machinery. Two simple examples demonstrate this. One is the driving, the overtaking— double and triple overtaking. Chinese drivers are not as exposed to the destructive power of motor vehicles as people are in the West through TV and police campaigns. Another example is of a young driver who drove his new car right over a huge rock that was in the middle of the road. The fuel dial swung downwards and a trail of fuel flowed out on to the roadway. He was quite surprised when the car stopped suddenly. He was so inexperienced that he just didn't imagine such a thing could happen. Anyone with experience would have taken evasive action.

In the case study the person delegated to get the water sample had no real understanding of the problems his deception would create for the quality of the product. What he did know was something more immediate: that if the village lost the plant because of the poor water quality, there would be trouble. The person who needed to calculate the dose of chemical to put into the tank didn't know how to carry out this simple calculation. This is not surprising, because the plant was located in the countryside where most locals had probably not gone beyond primary school. The solution devised by the Western manager is close supervision and with the opportunity given to the Chinese staff member to withdraw from a task in a face-saving manner.

Status

The phenomenon of the 'little chiefs' created by the training programs is a natural outcome of the Chinese social structure. Western expatriates in China since the earliest days of the nineteenth century remarked on the way their domestic staffs built little empires, the chief among them taking a part of the wages of all the other domestic servants. The Chinese themselves describe their relationships with others as a 'spider's web', each giving or taking nourishment from others.

Status was typically derived from education, leisure and a vast number of underlings. Education is prized because it is in short supply, thus leaving many people to do menial tasks. A group of Western construction supervisors observed the way Chinese middle managers exercised their status. They removed themselves from the workforce, stayed in their offices and 'supervised' from there. Any direction from the Western supervisors intended for the workers went all the way around middle management and got back to the workers two weeks later. The Western supervisors had to devise a short-circuit system so that they could get their directions straight to the workers without all the protocol that goes with issuing directions through middle management.

12

Supervision

In December 1937 the Japanese army occupied Nanjing, seat of the Nationalist government of China under Chiang Kai-shek. To protect the Chinese civilians from the atrocities of the Japanese soldiers, the manager of Siemens China Company, John Rabe, created an international safety zone. Into this zone crammed 250 000 Chinese. The Siemens compound itself sheltered 600 civilians. When the Japanese command were pressing Rabe to abandon the compound, 70 girls and women went on their knees and banged their heads against the ground, saying over and over: 'You are our father and our mother. You have protected us till now, don't stop half-way! If we are going to be violated and have to die, then we want to die here!' (Rabe 1998, p. 171)

At New Year his servants and employees and the refugees stood in rows, bowed to him three times and presented him with a scroll extolling him as the 'Living Buddha' because of his work in protecting them from the Japanese. These physical actions—bowing, kneeling and banging the head on the ground—are traditional manifestations of the boss–subordinate relationship: the superior above, the subordinate below. They were used again during the Democracy Movement in Tiananmen

Square in 1989 when student leaders presented their petition to the government: on their knees, heads bowed, the petition held aloft in both hands in symbolic presentation from subordinate to superior. And this occurred after a communist education!

These examples illustrate a relationship with 'the boss' that's rather different in form and expectation from the boss–subordinate relationship in most Western countries. Here the boss is elevated, his underlings on their knees below him. In return the boss has the responsibility, as had traditional Chinese officials, of being 'father and mother' to their subordinates. Another measure of the distance between boss and subordinate is the form of communication described in Chapter 4.

Western managers tread a fine line between being dictatorial, which is not well tolerated by local staff, and needing to show strength in order to maintain discipline. The hatred stirred up among the Chinese for certain types of dictatorial expatriate managers was brought up by many of the interviewees. One said, 'If they don't like you, you've got trouble'. The Chinese have a certain perception of the way a boss should treat them, and when this is transgressed, Westerners can feel the hostility of people whose own country China is, where they themselves are outsiders.

I took a lesson in how an atmosphere of maximum co-operation is built with Chinese workers when my Chinese landlady was building a block of flats right alongside the one we lived in. She often had the supervisor in for drinks and eats, flattering him mightily. She also put on a banquet for the labourers at certain stages during the construction process. Tables and stools were set out on the concrete floor of the partly finished building. Plenty of beer was supplied, and the landlady visited once or twice during the festivities to share a joke with them and see that they were all enjoying themselves.

A Western construction manager learned the benefit of such generosity by mistake. He invited the Chinese managers to a banquet, and somehow the invitation was extended to the workers—all 40 of them. They turned up and had a terrific time. The Chinese managers had the prestigious seats at the front of the restaurant; the workers had the back. From that time on his workers were not only co-operative but they guarded the expatriate group's tools and equipment so there was never any theft. The equipment of other expatriate groups was pilfered on a regular basis.

The nature of Chinese management is detailed here by the only expatriate manager in a manufacturing plant in south China: 'I'm not so much a manager as a father of an extended family. I'm invited to banquets, weddings, farewells, hospital visits, karaoke parties, table tennis matches, you name it. And that means being available many hours of the day and some nights. The staff and I will solve a crisis together and then go out ten pin bowling.' (Harris 1997, p. 26)

Here we have an apparent dilemma about how a Western manager should relate to Chinese employees: on the one hand, he or she must give directions, supervise closely and maintain discipline; while also, on the other hand, establishing a warm relationship. Dr George Renwick, a leading US cross-cultural consultant, typified the ideal Western manager for China as one 'with the heart of an educator'. A Chinese manager commenting on one of the expatriate managers at Volkswagen in Shanghai said, 'Although personally rather strict, he endeavours to come close to other people's ideas. Local workers find him always scolding and pushing; however they still feel he is reasonable' (Hoon-Halbauer 1996). So there is some latitude.

In the following case study of an international food manufacturer and marketer in Beijing, we see again the key management strategy of clear and accountable systems, and close management supervision. The manager has learned it by trial and error in the Chinese context.

Case study: 'Like a policeman'

'I started off using the same democratic style as at home, but I realised I was just wasting time. Our company structures here in China are hierarchical with clearly delineated power and responsibilities. If you use less clearly defined methods, nothing is achieved. We used to talk about things for a long time and nothing ever happened. Finally we realised, "This is crazy". Then we started saying to people, "Okay just do this".

'They run decisions up the management hierarchy. In the end the general manager is making decisions about where the photocopier should be. I have to say, "I am not going to make a decision about this. You have to go away and sort it out for yourselves". Time was being whittled away by trivial things. There is a huge amount of time taken in recruiting staff, and in inter-departmental disputes. I have to say, "You either work it out yourselves or I won't require either of you next week", meaning, "You won't have a job next week".'

He has to constantly check up and monitor, in his words, 'like a policeman'. His salesforce was instructed to call on stores a certain number of times a week to check that the stores had a core range of his company's products. For each store there is a simple form to be filled out. He could tell from the way the forms were completed that the figures weren't correct. So he went out to check on the work himself, something he believes 'the general manager should not be doing'. He took the form, went to the store and checked it, then the same to another twenty stores—the figures were all wrong. He gave the salesforce a warning about this issue.

He tried for three months to convince them of the importance of having evaluations of what products were in what stores, explaining the reasons behind it. He told the salesforce, 'I don't care what the result is, but I want the figures to be accurate. Then we will know whether we are progressing or going backward. I don't care what the result is, as long as we have accurate scores.' But they thought he wanted a good result, so no matter what the figures were, they falsified them to look good.

Ultimate consequences

After this he gave the sales management, from the national manager to the local city managers, a final warning about the forms. If they got them wrong again, they would be dismissed. He said to them, 'Tomorrow I am going to the stores that you have said have our core range and I am going to check them. You've got one day to give me the accurate answer.' They came back with the true answer the next day: not one of the stores had the core range.

He says of his direct management approach, 'It sounds like a sledge-hammer method, but we had to get this right. This determines what distribution we have in our stores. It is crucial data. They hated it because the data was measurable. You have to pay attention to detail. You must put in a system that measures key drivers in the business. Each manager has to sign off on the forms. Each person is accountable for what they do. It's a powerful thing. It's not "we nearly had it" or "we had it yesterday".

'In the past if you asked the national sales manager or the local sales manager, "What's the distribution of the product like?" they would say, "It's good." I'd say, "How do you know it's good?" "I checked the stores, and it's good." "Better than last month?" "Yes." But there was no system to really tell me whether sales were good or not. Now we can tell each month.'

Comment

The boss–staff relationship

Here we have an example of a Chinese tendency to tell the boss what he wants to hear. There are a number of ways to account for this. One is the reasoning process. There is research evidence that Chinese people, when given a decision task, are more positive about the outcomes than Westerners. When generating arguments about a course of action they need to decide on, they produce more 'pros' than 'cons'. Researchers have attributed this confidence to Chinese teaching and learning styles, rather than to personal overconfidence. The Chinese teaching style is based on models that students then emulate. This contrasts with Western education in which students are valued for their own opinions, write essays and take part in debates during which they formulate lists of 'pros' and 'cons'. Western judicial systems use confrontation, challenge and debate to reach a solution. Chinese systems use mediation, conciliation and guided solutions. Chinese students are therefore not exposed to compiling lists of 'pros' and 'cons', and thus are not trained to produce a list of negatives (Yates and Lee 1996). It is quite possible that in many of these situations they haven't adequately considered the negative outcomes from their actions, and proceed on what we would consider to be 'overconfidence'.

Another factor is the power and status of the boss. In the ideal boss–subordinate relationship the subordinate wants to please the boss. The proper order in a hierarchical society like China is that the person with the highest status makes the decision or makes clear his or her wishes, and subordinates act in accord with those wishes. However, the negative aspect is that bosses have great power over the personal and working lives of employees—in both traditional family businesses and under the communist state enterprise system. Fear of displeasing the boss means that bad news is hidden from him or her. This was plainly evident in the Maoist period when cadres (officials) falsified agricultural and industrial production statistics to meet or exceed targets set by the central government. Falsification of statistics is still happening, and the central authorities have issued stern warnings to local officials against the practice.

The really interesting thing about the reporting problem in this case study is that, although clear and straightforward systems had been introduced, and their purpose explained thoroughly, the manager still had to go around the shops himself checking that the figures were correct. He had to ultimately come to the point of threatening staff with dismissal before he was able to get them to adopt a Western analytical approach, irrespective of its relationship to the boss. Threats, such as the one he used to fire the staff, are a well-known tactic in negotiation theory. Called 'ultimate consequences', the tactic is used to signal the bottom line, the furthest extent to which a person is prepared to be pushed. This tactic seems to be used frequently by Western managers in China.

Directive, hands-on supervision

The Western manager is worried about his 'sledgehammer' style, so different from how he used to operate in his company's head office. There he was used to democratic decision-making, consultation, delegation and self-reliance. There is a lot of evidence that this Western style is not successful in China. A study of foreign management difficulties in China (Child 1991) found that while Western managers had trouble with Chinese staff in decision-making, systematic approaches, communication and training, Hong Kong managers mentioned these difficulties least. The greatest difference was that the Western managers were introducing wholesale change, while the Hong Kong managers were not. Hong Kong managers were using the 'command and obey' system.

The foreign general managers in the case studies in this part of the book have had to redefine the tasks of a general manager in China. Close supervision is the key among them. The same redefinition is recounted by many Western expatriates. An air-conditioning expert explains how his experience in China changed the way he managed: 'I worked a lot closer with the workers on my second assignment in China. I tried harder to help them, to get along with them and to have a bit of fun with them, not just giving them directions all the time. I enjoyed it a lot more, and I think they did too. I played basketball and soccer with them. I had a few jokes with them and told them if they did anything wrong, I'd turn them into astronauts. They saw the humour in it. They had all learned English at school but a lot of them were very afraid of speaking it in case they made a mistake. But by the end they were talking to us in English. The biggest problem is that our workers were not trained in the industry. My head pipe guy was a school teacher; the head electrician was a concreter. So we had skilled people but not in our areas.'

Hands-on management consumes a lot of time. Very few head office executives understand this. Because there is so much training of staff to be done in China, many managers and technical experts, feeling the time pressure from head office, find it faster and more efficient to fix problems themselves, rather than delegate it to Chinese staff and then implement a detailed follow-up. This 'quick fix' solution prevents Chinese staff acquiring the necessary skills. A key question for expatriates to ask themselves is: 'What is your primary mission?' 1. To get the job and tasks done? or 2. To enable the Chinese to get the job done? (Fallon 1997).

At least the manager in this case study is attempting to overcome the temptation to fix things himself, by passing problems back to the staff for their solution. However, he has to deal with the pressures from his own head office, yet another educational task for him. He said, 'What we achieve is never enough for head office. Their expectations are based on an unfair comparison. It's like comparing a high school sprinter with an Olympic champion. It's like saying, "Why can't you run that speed? What's the issue? We're putting just as much money into your training, so why are you only running at high school speed, and these other people are running at Olympic speed?"' This is the difficulty of operating in an environment of such difference from home.

13

Manager quality

Sometimes, by great good fortune, a company comes across someone who is not only a good manager, but who also has a heart for the Chinese people. Earlier in the book I quoted the American Russell & Co. who looked for clerks able to relate well to the Chinese (Chapter 4). Some companies have also confided that their choice of manager was inappropriate because of the manager's inability to relate well to the Chinese and that this caused business problems. Managers able to combine the skills that are appropriate for the challenges of China—such as leadership, control, transfer of knowledge and effective communication—with a positive emotional relationship to the Chinese are what is required. By 'positive emotional relationship' I don't mean those people commonly said to have 'gone native', abandoning Western standards of business and adopting local standards in their place. Rather, I mean people who are realistic, who maintain their focus on good practice, and who bring Chinese employees to that level through a sympathetic regard for the local culture.

Such people are helped to be successful by the situation in which the parent company places them. If the investment strategy is well thought through using local knowledge as the base, then the task of the Western manager is far easier than when he or she is struggling in an unwinable situation. The next case study brings all these elements into sharp focus. The speaker is the operations manager of a 70–30 Western–Chinese joint venture garment factory in Beijing.

Case study: 'A bowl of lollies'

'In 1985 I went to China to do some training at the No. 1 Sock Factory in Beijing. It was a state-owned enterprise. I would be teaching in the knitting room and the general manager, the chief engineer, the designer and other top managers would spend the day playing mahjong.

'One night I couldn't sleep. I got up and took a taxi to the factory. The guard was asleep in the guard house. I let myself in. In the factory I was stepping over bodies—they were sleeping all over the floor. Only six of the 60 machines were running. It was meant to be a 24-hour operation. There were three people working of the 40 or so who were on that shift.

'The next day I spoke to the manager of the section. She replied, "You are here to *teach*, not to criticise!" So I said I wanted to speak to Mr Jiang, the general manager. He knew me well. He said, "I can't do anything about it".

'That company had 1400 workers, and they were making 2000 dozen socks per day. In our company at home we would make 3000 dozen socks and 2000 units of women's singlets with 350 workers. I wrote a report for my company. I said that the No. 1 Sock Factory could never be changed. I advised my bosses to set up our own factory. Now the No. 1 Sock Factory is closed. All the workers lost their jobs.

'I started our factory in Beijing in 1986 with ten Chinese to help me. Five of those people are still with me. I lived in an old Chinese hotel where all the peasants used to come and stay overnight for 1 RMB (about 16 cents), six beds to a room. All the children would toddle up to look at me. I used to have a bowl of lollies to spoil them. In our factory now I have 103 grandchildren. They say, "Hello, grandfather".

'I lived in that Chinese hotel for four years. I had a TV and video, a bedroom, a loungeroom and a boardroom. That was all. I spent a lot of time setting up the factory. The hours didn't mean anything. I would stay in the factory training the workers until ten or eleven at night and the group of people around me grew very close to me. I visited their homes, all types of homes—from very poor homes to better-class homes. I met their parents.'

Establishing control

'Although it is a joint venture, our company runs it and we select the staff. On a number of occasions the Chinese partner wanted to put in assistant general managers to me. We said "no". We will not have an assistant general manager who is a Chinese person in the factory. If they did that, he or she could create havoc with the Chinese people. They've been managing Chinese factories. Their ideas are not like our ideas. You would have a person saying, "My boss doesn't like this. We should do this". One day there will be a Chinese general manager, but he will be appointed by our company, not by the Chinese.

'I am entirely different from their Chinese bosses. I know that because I had the privilege of working in the No. 1 Sock Factory. I know about the "iron rice bowl" mentality. Their managers spent little time with the workers. They didn't know what was going on. When a problem arose, they couldn't handle it. I see myself as the hub of the wheel and we are all going round together.

'In the early days at board meetings there would be fourteen Chinese directors and two expatriates. Our company has 70 per cent equity. They'd all smoke. We couldn't do anything. They'd sit there for five or six hours and nothing was achieved. Now our board meetings only take two hours, and we only have the Chinese chairman and two others apart from two expatriates. And we have a "No smoking" sign.'

Managing

'There is a language barrier and a method barrier to managing in China. We sent a group of fifteen people to university to learn English. They learned it very well, except for Mr Bai. He said he was wasting his time and asked not to continue. Mr Bai has the most wonderful heart. He'll walk into my room (I live at the factory) and I'll say, "Have a beer, Mr Bai". I give him a beer and an ashtray. We won't say five or six words in twenty minutes. He'll drink his beer, say, "Goodnight" and away he goes. In the old days the power used to go off. One night it suddenly went off. Soon there's a knock at the door and Mr Bai, Madame Jiang and all the supervisors come into our room. My wife and myself were in bed. It was pitch black. They sat on the bed and said, "Teach us English". So my wife and myself got up and we all talked to one another in English. There was a challenge between them about who was going to be the best in their English course. They all got about 95–96 per cent, except Mr Bai who dropped out.

'We only employ people who have not worked in state enterprises. They don't have bad work habits. You can teach them. If they are no good, it is my fault. We do a lot of training. I find it easy to train Chinese people. I've been there so long, but I cannot speak Chinese. Everybody knows me—they know my sign language. They know me very, very well. I don't have to speak. They know when I am upset—when my eyes are flashing. They work on piece-work. The more units they produce, the more money they can earn. We assess them on quality. They are no different from workers in our home company. Sometimes they let a sock that isn't up to standard slip through. If they make the same mistake two or three times they're penalised. They lose half of their bonus. They work in groups of three. Each group is responsible for a group of machines. I make the group pay, not the individual, because it is the effort of three people. The first person should have seen that product fault, then the others missed it. They all fail, they all lose a percentage of their bonus, so they make sure next time that they do the job properly.

'I get mad when they do something stupid. They've got the knowledge, but they are lax occasionally. They don't think. If the worker comes up with a suggestion or a question, the managers just say, "You can't do that", without looking into the problem. That is when I blow up. If the work is bad, I hold the manager of the department responsible. I thump the table. Then they know. They back off. After five minutes they'll say, "Mr Jack, you still angry?" I'll say "no" and give them a smile. I can criticise and they take it. After that it's over. But with their own Chinese people they will go against them for days and days.

'Many times I have had to intervene when they have bad relations among themselves. I have to act like a father. Some managers hate to tell their workers off. If they have friends working in the same department, they cannot discipline them. They will say, "we are sisters", or "we are friends". Sometimes the interpreter will not interpret correctly. Although I don't speak Chinese I know when they are not translating correctly. You can tell from the body language or the expression on the other person's face.

'Communication causes a lot of headaches. If I want to talk to a person, I speak to the department manager and tell him what I am doing. Otherwise, if you talk to the worker, he is likely to tell the manager a totally different story. Then the manager says, "He's interfering in my department".

'The worker can also give the wrong interpretation to the manager. The manager can give the wrong interpretation to the worker. A common one is, "Jack doesn't like what you are doing", when I haven't said that. One day a woman in the knitting room said to me, "I'm angry with you". I said, "Why? What have I done?" "You told the manager I am no good." I said, "What are you talking about?" He had twisted the message. I told her, "When I am unhappy about something I look you in the eyes and say, 'You are not doing your job properly'. I don't go and tell someone to tell you that I think you are no good".

'The manager had tried to save his own face. He didn't have the stomach to say it all out. I had said, "These people aren't doing their job properly". The manager had twisted it to, "Jack's not happy. He thinks you are no good".

'I have had people I've had to get rid of. Once it was the chief engineer's son. I put him on, against my better judgment, because of pressure from his father. He often took time off. One day he deliberately broke a bottle on the basketball court. I made him sweep it up. His father offered "payola" to keep him on. I said, "No, I'm sorry". They all knew I had discipline. It was very important for them to see that.

'We give instant dismissal for thieving and fighting. In other cases we give them a reprimand. The second time they get a dismissal. You can make it unpleasant without hurting their feelings. Of our 350 people, 125 have been here for over eight years. The young modern ones sometimes don't really want to work, but there are no unemployment benefits in China. They work for a couple of days, get a bit of pocket money, then they report "sick". Their mum and dad look after them—that's the effect of the one child policy.

'We have a production meeting every Monday with the department managers. The general manager says what the aim is, what the budget is, what we have to do to get the production target. Each person is asked what their problem is. We make them run the meeting and we sit and listen. Everyone has to give his or her report. The general manager puts the questions: "Why . . . ", "Have you looked into . . . ". When we first started, the Chinese managers would sit there and not say anything. We'd generally find out the problem three days later. You'd come out of the meeting thinking everything is okay, no problems! Three days later everything collapses around your neck.

'In the state-controlled factories they give them "model worker" banners. We never do that. The greatest way to cause discontent in a factory is to say, "He's a model worker". Everyone else thinks, "What's he done that I don't do?" In our factory, people who are proficient are rewarded with a bonus. They think money is more important than the title "model worker".

'Our workers are very conscientious, very clever. They learn very quickly. If any of the people who work for our company buy our product they will not accept a slightly crooked seam. That's when they are buying—they are very quality-conscious. Sometimes when they are producing they aren't quite so quality-conscious!'

Relating

'Normally I rise at 4 am. At 6 am I go to the factory, to the dyehouse, pressroom, toe closing section, knitting room. I poke around, talk to people about their problems. I'm like a father to them. We have a dormitory, hot and cold showers, meals. At least three times a week I eat in the canteen. I like people to know that I am prepared to sit down with them. The cooks know that I comment on the meals.

'We have three shifts: 8 am to 4 pm, 4 pm to midnight, and midnight to 8 am. As progress comes to China, so does crime. Violence is surfacing. A lot of the women stay overnight in the dormitory for a small charge instead of going home in the dark, or if they are on the midnight to 8 am shift. In the morning they can have a hot shower, hop on their bike and ride home.

'When a container of machines came they pushed me out, "You rest, you rest". In the workshop they'll push me aside, "We'll do this". They call me "Lao Jacka", "Old Mr Jack". On the weekend I go out with the Chinese, fishing, picnicking, swimming in the lakes or in the big sports centre with the water slides and artificial waves. Recently we took 300 employees up to the "Ten Bridges" in the mountains. They were booked into five different lodgings. It was a really happy weekend—horseriding, paddleboating, swimming.

'I say I have given birth to a factory. I've nourished it and looked after it. I never forget my people who have stuck by me. When I first came to China everyone wore blue Mao suits buttoned up to the neck. Since then a great transformation has taken place. One of the girls in the factory even has blond hair. I wondered who the new girl was. It was one of the regular staff—she'd dyed her hair!

'When I had a bad knee I had about fourteen people all bringing different medicines, rubbing them into my knee. Mr Bai wanted to stay the night, to sleep in my room. I don't mix much with other expatriates. I've got so many Chinese friends, and I have a great deal of love for them as they've been kind to me. It is a real working relationship which has been a very happy one. If I've been working flat out with the engineers or the packers, they'll not have had dinner. They'll come and say, "We go to restaurant, Jack", and haul me off.

'My advice is to understand their culture—that way, they will like you. I've seen them work sixteen to seventeen hours to get an order out. But if they don't like you, you've got trouble. They are just as intelligent as we are. Never underestimate them. They are human beings who should be treated fairly and justly at all times. Mix with them, have a beer with them, go to their weddings, eat with them in the little old restaurant. This is friendship. I spent yesterday shopping for all the people who gave me presents for my 65th birthday. They gave me long life Buddhas, silk, materials for shirts and trousers . . .'

Comment

The reality

Jack's company used a wise strategy for its entry to manufacturing in China. They sent him there to work in a state-owned enterprise before they made any commitment. He saw the socialist industrial scene at first hand and assessed it as unchangeable. As a result, his company avoided the management entanglement documented in many other case studies. The company made a modest start in a new factory on a greenfield site. They had to be in a joint venture, according to the Chinese law of the time. They had dominant equity of 70 per cent to the Chinese 30 per cent. However, the 70 per cent equity did not protect them from the old Chinese ways at board meetings. Chinese directors dominated the board, and meetings wasted valuable expatriate time. Although the board had Chinese directors, the internal management of the factory was placed in the hands of their own people and they strongly resisted the pressure to appoint a Chinese deputy general manager. Jack rightly anticipated that this would split worker loyalty and end up in conflict at management level.

Management control within the joint venture structure was achieved only after senior management spent months talking it through with the local bureaus and the joint venture partner. The company was also under sustained pressure to employ people recommended by the labour bureau and the partner. This also necessitated months of negotiations during which they emphasised to the bureau officials that their aim was profitability, and the bureaus would benefit from that in time. Their main strategy was export—and that gave them negotiation strength, since boosting exports was a key government priority. As time went on and they became very profitable, pressure from the bureaus eased. The joint venture company now sells into the Chinese market, but export is still a major strategy. Their export success made it easier to change such things as the dominance of the board by old-style Chinese directors. This has now been streamlined and meetings are effective and efficient.

Expatriate quality

Just as the company's entry strategy was wisely devised, so too was their choice of the expatriate operations manager. Most expatriates cost their companies a great deal of money in allowances, accommodation, family arrangements, membership of country clubs and recreation out of China. Jack was adaptable and did not live an expatriate life separated from Chinese workers. His accommodation was modest in the old Chinese hotel first and later in the flat attached to the factory.

He had affection and respect for the Chinese. His age may well have contributed to this attitude. He was in his late fifties when he went to China. He wasn't on the management ladder to somewhere else. His whole attention was focused on his task in China—to set up the factory and get its production systems running at world best practice. He brought with him years of experience in production and the management of workers. The Chinese authorities have publicly spoken against foreign companies sending close-to-retirement or retirees to manage their China investments. They want young people who they see as being more at the cutting edge of technological expertise. However, young people do not necessarily have the management skills to deal with the current Chinese situation.

Jack rarely mixed with other expatriates. He saw the Chinese as his friends and spent both his work and leisure time with them. He had the time to put into training. The hours he put in at the factory were a pleasure and not a pressure.

All these elements—his age, his commitment, his affection for Chinese people, his modest lifestyle—won him a positive response from the employees. It wasn't weakness that made people like him. In fact, he was tough. He was consistent, and he didn't put a barrier between himself and the employees as so many expatriate managers do through living separately and pursuing an expensive lifestyle.

Organisation

It is said that the majority of Chinese employees like a directive leader. Jack was certainly clear in his mind about what was required in organisation and discipline. He used small groups as the basis of the production system, a strategy that would appear to suit Chinese collectivist preferences. Discipline, in the form of bonuses and penalties on the bonus, was group-based at the worker level.

The managers received extensive training in production, management and English. They were also closely monitored. Jack paid respect to their position by always going through the chain of command when there was a problem in the department. Without a split Chinese–Western management at the top level, Jack was able to have management authority over the department managers. Control mechanisms were thus clear. This contrasts with the two expatriate managers in the glass mould factory in Chapter 10 whose directions were secretly countermanded by the parallel Chinese managers—a situation foreseen by Jack in regard to his own factory.

All staff were recruited by the factory and put on probation. Once when Jack sidestepped this system to appoint the son of the chief engineer, he had to wear the consequences of the boy's deliberate challenge to his authority. Jack immediately picked the game and made an example of the boy by making him clean up the broken glass and then dismissing him.

Earlier in the book I quoted Dr George Renwick's description of the ideal expatriate manager in China as one 'with the heart of an educator'. Clear discipline is as much in the hearts of educators as the passing on of knowledge. This seems to fit in with the Chinese preference in organisations for a strong leader. Western managers are trying to insert something that is more Western than Chinese—the self-reliant middle manager. This is a difficult task and Jack points to some of the issues when he says that department managers, when asked for a decision by shop floor workers, give an easy answer without thinking the problem through. He said, 'They don't think. It's something I've only met in China.' What might be a more accurate assessment than 'they don't think', is 'they are reluctant to take responsibility for a decision that could result in a negative outcome'. People who are used to the command-and-obey model of management are also used to punishment when things go wrong. In a Chinese family this would be a public shaming. From the Chinese point of view, taking responsibility publicly for a decision could also result in public humiliation if it doesn't work. Such managers need a lot of support from top management to act according to the Western middle management model.

The factory provides benefits for workers, much as the old state enterprises do, and thus fits in with the Chinese workers' expectations of their employing company.

Communication and meetings

Language is a significant barrier to management effectiveness in China. Jack acknowledges this, despite his use of 'flashing eyes', 'blowing up' and 'thumping on the table'. Giving the Chinese department managers English-language training was an early and effective strategy. Their English, though, is still not at native-speaker level—quite naturally, since they have never lived abroad. They misinterpret and misunderstand the tone of what is said. This hinders mutual understanding. Such misunderstandings are hard to avoid and to trace, but their effect is obvious—such as the woman who was told that Jack thought she was 'no good'. The actual command of the language is one impediment; another is what messages are acceptable for Chinese people.

Jack specifies the difficulty department managers have in supervising their staff when close relationships are involved. The managers do not like to discipline 'sisters' and 'friends'. They also recoil from saying plainly what the problem is. Jack observes closely and is aware of mistranslation. But even so, he says, 'communication causes a lot of headaches'. This is another reason for time to be given to management tasks in China. Communication cannot be accomplished so fast because of faulty English-language skills and the Chinese preference for indirectness.

The meeting procedure is a good example of indirectness in use. The managers don't like to be the bearers of bad news, and in the beginning the expatriate managers weren't aware of this. They would probably do most of the talking, and consequently missed really important issues known to the Chinese managers. Now their strategy is one of silence and helping the Chinese managers to communicate more openly about their problems.

One of Jack's key strengths is something advised in all management books—MBWA, or Management By Walking Around. Jack is obviously around and about the factory keeping a watchful eye on everything.

This is a positive story, but it is not a dream story. Prudence was used at the beginning and prudence is still necessary fourteen years later. The factory has regularly faced problems of production timing. About one-quarter of deliveries for the export market run a month late. Chinese solutions to technical problems can exacerbate the problems because they are not technologically appropriate and can damage the machines. Gaining appropriate supplies is an on-going challenge, and attracting and retaining skilled management staff has to be worked at continuously. On the Western side, some ill-advised decision-making has at times caused relationship problems with the joint venture partner and the local bureaus, such as the time the group director of China operations, an overseas Chinese, under-reported the profits made by the company on exports. It was a deliberate deception, and it is unfortunate that it marred an otherwise good relationship, much of it built on 'Old Mr Jack's' exemplary management practices. In the production area, the factory is at and sometimes exceeds world best practice.

IV

Bureaucracy and business

14

The socialist market economy

Although the market reforms have opened the way for private business, expatriate managers in China find that the market economy is not as market-determined as in the advanced economies. Some of the differences are described here by expatriate managers operating in different parts of China:

- 'It is a state-owned economy and the government believes it can interfere in the operation of your business at any time for no reason whatsoever.' (South China)
- 'We would like to be left alone to run our business and pay our taxes according to what we have agreed to do.' (Shanghai)
- 'The bureaucracy has the ability to unilaterally impose something on a business, retrospectively, and you have no right of redress.' (Tianjin)
- 'The bureaucracy is business. Everyone I'm exposed to is bureaucracy. We don't sell or buy from private concerns. My view is that the whole of China is bureaucracy. We are selling to government departments, and we interface with the bureaucracy in customs, employment and in many other areas.' (Various provinces)

Surveys conducted by the United States–China Business Council (1995, 1996, 1998) found that 'government interference' was a key problem for foreign-invested businesses.

Top-down legislation from the central government

Central government law-making in China is top-down, suddenly implemented and subject to rapid change. Information about proposed regulatory changes is rarely available to foreign enterprises, although such changes can have a huge impact on their operations and profitability. In the following case study, a manager in south China reports on one example of the central government issuing regulations without adequate consultation or preparation.

Case study: VAT

'The single biggest challenge is that having built our factory under a certain set of rules, all of a sudden the Chinese government changed the rules. This happened with a 17 per cent VAT. They didn't do anything about regulations and systems to make it work. It was decided in Beijing.

'Most of our competitors, and the Chinese government corporations, just ignored it. They'd open a shop-front somewhere and do all their dealings through that shop-front. When the government inspectors came along to investigate, they'd just close that down and move somewhere else. We were operating at a 17 per cent disadvantage, because as a foreign multinational company we expect to pay it. Now they've put in a system with monitoring. So, pretty much everyone is paying VAT.

'The central government has a horrible tendency to suddenly pass a law without any system for imposing it, making it work, checking on it, etc. The further away from Beijing, the less people worry about it. If you are caught, you are up for it anyway. If you are a legitimate foreign company you must comply as we do. You get VAT vouchers. You pay everything first, then you write a VAT voucher and the government pays you back.

'In the first year the government paid more back on the vouchers than they collected on the tax, because people falsified all these vouchers. They then started to impose some structure. They actually executed some people in southern China for VAT fraud. They just took them to the local village square and put a bullet in the back of their neck. That sorted a few people out. The VAT fraud is still going on, even though they've executed people.'

Comment

This manager expresses a concern felt by many Western executives at the government's lack of consultation with private business and a concern that a lack of infrastructure to implement the law fairly across all businesses can disadvantage foreign corporations vis-à-vis local companies because they must play 'according to the law', whereas local companies find ways to manoeuvre around the law.

It is not merely a contemporary phenomenon due to the market reform process that the government imposes new laws and regulations without consulting business people. In one example from 1880, a Chinese businessman in Hankow [Hankou] wrote to the *Shen pao* newspaper to complain about new regulations issued without consultation that forced ships on the Yangtze to make many stops to fill out a multiplicity of tax declarations. He advised the government that 'in the enactment of regulations, one should strive for simplicity and convenience, rather than vexatiousness and the imposition of impediments to trade. In enforcement, one should seek methods that are comprehensive and refined, rather than those based on petty grasping' (Mann 1987, pp. 185–6).

In the face of policy-making from the top, Chinese people have traditionally clustered together in self-protective and self-regulating groups based on a shared industry—guilds and chambers of commerce, or associations of native place (*tongxianghui*). They dealt with government in two ways: they represented the interests of their members to policy-makers, and they acted as tax collection agencies for the government. By negotiating tax rates with government officials they sought to protect their members from excessive taxation and forced contributions.

In Shanghai during the last century the commercial guilds followed the principle of 'non-political entanglement' to avoid entanglement with officials and the external court system. They set up their own regulations for members which were enforced by guild members. Commercial disputes among members were adjudicated within the guild (Goodman 1995).

The following case documents a successful strategy not unlike that of the traditional Chinese commercial guilds just mentioned. It was implemented by foreign businesses when the central government suddenly imposed a law that all imports of plant and equipment for new or existing foreign-invested ventures were to pay a surcharge of 25–40 per cent from a certain date. The reaction was strong and co-ordinated because the new law had a dramatic negative effect on the future competitiveness of foreign business. Strategic plans and feasibility studies were turned on their head because companies would need to add up to 40 per cent to the value of their imported equipment.

Case study: The 40 per cent surcharge

'This sudden surcharge caused a lot of angst in our head office as to whether or not the investment should go ahead, whether or not the feasibilities had to be redone, and the whole economic viability of the project. What occurred was a massive amount of lobbying by companies individually and in groups through their embassies or chambers of commerce in Beijing. The mass lobbying has led to companies being able to convince the government that on normal international rules one would not just impose a cut-off next week.

'The result of this was that the authorities in Beijing allowed time in which companies that already had preliminary approvals or final approvals could go to the authorities and say, "This is the deal: we negotiated on this basis, with this tax structure, we've been approved, we spent a lot of time and energy on getting to this point in terms of overheads—we should get the exemption." So the government set in place a procedure whereby you could take your proposals case by case, get them stamped off, and import your equipment up to a certain date. It gave companies a window of opportunity to process their proposals for investment according to their original thinking.

'I think this lack of consultation with domestic or foreign companies has something to do with the way the regulatory machine runs in Beijing. A lot of issues are decided in-house. Things have been moving so quickly that the government hasn't yet set up the mature consultation channels, processes and procedures whereby it can sit down with strategic investors and say, "OK, what is your thinking on it?" before they hit the panic button.

'Foreign-invested corporations are simply not used to this treatment, because in the West they get consulted along the way, so you own the policy by the time it comes in. People come and talk to you, "We've got this problem, we would like to instigate this net to get . . . " Companies say, "Oh, I understand where you are coming from. How about you do this or do that?" People own the thing before it gets up. But in China it tends to be whoosh! You're in and that's it. You don't have much say.'

Comment

In the case of the 40 per cent surcharge, foreign companies found it effective to lobby as industry groups, rather than as single companies. Usually the government will not deal with the complaints of individual companies. Lobbying at the political level through embassies representing national relations with the Chinese government, as well as through purely business-focused industry groupings, added strength to their cause. Such a proactive, jointly organised approach in dealing with central government regulations is a useful strategy, (a) because it mirrors China's own tradition of government interaction with groups representing business interests, and (b) because regulations are always open to negotiation, even after promulgation.

15

Local government power

So foreign investors have concerns about top-down law-making without consultation with business. As well as that they must deal with local governments whose officers exercise discretion in the interpretation of laws and regulations. Local laws are often inconsistent with central laws, and there are differences in legal interpretation and administrative directives.

One manager described the situation. 'The problem raised by foreigners is the inconsistent enforcement of laws and regulations that emanate from Beijing. It's not uncommon to find that despite the fact that foreign investors have basically a uniform national tax treatment, with the exception of special economic zones, when it gets down to talking with the local tax authorities you find that their interpretation of the regulations is different from place to place. So if you have joint ventures in Tianjin, Guangzhou and Shanghai, you'll find that you have different treatment, different procedures, different rates applying in the three areas.'

Underlying this complaint are two misconceptions: that China is a unity, rather than a geographically and politically diverse collection of provinces; and that the Chinese legal system has a similar foundation to British-derived legal–political systems. In fact, the modern legal system of China incorporates features of the Napoleonic Code which distinguishes it from the British system.

As in France, Chinese law recognises the principle of entrusted or inherent power. That is, that laws are broadly drafted at the central level, but rule-making and implementation based on those laws is left to the discretion of the lower levels of the bureaucracy. As long as an administrative organisation does not go beyond its specific mandate, it has legislative power to draft and enact legislation to govern its own area of responsibility. Thus, government departments and provincial governments have both administrative and legislative power, unlike in English-speaking countries where these powers are separated. Chinese administrative bodies are granted 'virtually unlimited rulemaking discretion' so long as their rule-making is not contrary to 'the spirit of' applicable law and the Constitution (Corne 1997, p. 56). Wang Hanbin, when director of the Judicial Committee to the National People's Congress, said: 'law should not be too specific lest it tie our hands and feet in the face of the rapidly changing situation' (Corne 1997, p. 94). This very approach to the role of law has led foreign investors to complain about the general uncertainty that surrounds the drafting, enactment and amendment of administrative laws, regulations and rules, the lack of opportunity for industry input and the law's inherent changeability (Corne 1997, p. 53).

Local governments derive their authority entirely from the central government. To balance this power of the centre, great flexibility is allowed to local governments. The Organic Law of Local People's Congresses and Local People's Governments allows enactment of laws 'according to concrete local conditions and actual needs' (Corne 1997, p. 83).

A Chinese scholar, Zhu Xinmin, has explained the relationship between central law, local interpretation and the powers of bureaucrats from a Chinese point of view.

'. . . the country is too big in terms of both population and territory, and too diverse in terms of both

folkways and customs, for the Central government to enact any uniform and clear-cut ordinance on the whole nation . . . the Central government always decides on a regulation in principle and instructs provincial governments, Central ministries and big firms to issue the corresponding regulation in concrete, so as to adapt the Central principles to each local, specific condition. Thus exceptions are allowed to almost all Central government regulations. The same is true even of relations between a province and its municipalities and medium-sized firms. In this context any prominent administrator . . . is in a position to give a go-ahead to an exception . . . and can find out a suitable reason for it, such as to relieve rural poverty, to reduce losses incurred by a state-owned firm, or to defuse disturbances among a group of employees.'
(Zhu 1996, p. 276)

Officials use their discretionary local power to advantage their income-gathering, even though their actions may be at odds with central government policies and laws. For example, it is the policy of the central government to limit the amount of imported equipment and materials used in foreign-invested enterprises to force localisation of supply and retain foreign currency. Notwithstanding this policy, when agreements with foreign business people are to local advantage, the 'spirit' of central policies can be reinterpreted. A multinational manufacturer in south China made an agreement under which the more material was imported, the more money the local mayor and his bureaucracy made.

'We negotiated with the Economic Co-operation Committee that we would have a contract of fee-for-service,' explained a foreign negotiator experienced in assessing Chinese needs. 'We would pay a percentage on the value of every ton of raw material we imported for our business. So the better we ran and the more raw material we imported, the more money they got. It was a fraction of a per cent—very small. That was a pretty good way of ensuring on-going co-operation.'

The British American Tobacco Company (BAT), a multinational corporation which has manufactured and distributed cigarettes in China since before 1949, used the discretion given to central and local bureaucrats to gain a competitive advantage for itself. It negotiated special tax rates that advantaged it over local Chinese tobacco companies. In 1915 BAT contracted with central and provincial governments for a tax of $2 per case, while Chinese brands paid between $3 and $10 per case. In Shansi [Shanxi] province, due to BAT negotiations with local officials, BAT cigarettes were exempt from tax while Chinese cigarettes were taxed at $15 per case. As a result of such 'contracting', BAT's tax burden in China was light and its resulting profits high (Cochran 1980, pp. 73, 128).

Under China's traditional imperial system of government, the centre maintained a certain distance by delegating many of its powers to groups that operated as 'go-betweens', between the government and the people. Tax collection, policing, and many controls on business were delegated to local bodies. At the very centre, the Emperor was counselled to share his power.

'Compliantly he delegates affairs to his subordinates and without troubling himself exacts success from them . . . thus he rides upon the power of the multitude as though it were his carriage, drives the wisdom of the multitude as though it were his horse, and though he traverse dark plains and steep roads, he will never go astray . . . there is nothing in the whole world that he does not comprehend, for those who come to report to him are many, and those who survey for him are numerous.' (From Huai-nan Tzu, 9:1a, 6b–7a, a collection of essays written or compiled by scholars at the court of Liu An d. 122 BC. Prince of Huai-nan and grandson of Kao-tsu, the first emperor of the Han— De Bary et al. 1960, p. 174) This system is well in evidence today.

A tradition in the appointment of officials under the imperial system was called 'the law of avoidance'. No official was permitted to serve in his home district because of the overwhelming pressure to favour local interests over national interests. This sense of locality was so strong that special administrative means had to be used to control it. Over a 257-year period from 1644 to 1901, district magistrates were moved to new posts on average every two-and-a-half years to prevent bonds forming with local interests (Chang 1955). Most Western business people would testify to the strength of local interests in contemporary China.

Local government power always needs to be factored into the forecasts and projections foreign companies make in China. If their projections are based only on the national treatment of foreign-invested enterprises, companies will find their projections falsified by new taxes and levies imposed by local and municipal authorities. In the two case studies that follow, expatriates explain the variety of additional local taxes.

Case study: Relocation tax for returned servicemen

'We have been paying a local tax in Shanghai relating to relocation fees for returned servicemen. This issue was raised about the time of the military exercises off the coast of China near the province of Taiwan. To my way of thinking, returned servicemen's entitlements shouldn't really be a local issue. The defence of the country is pretty much a central government activity, and we were being asked by the Shanghai authorities to make a contribution to this fund. We have done so. We felt that we should simply make the contribution and keep our heads down.

'It wasn't a huge amount of money. It was a tax on the amount of tax you already paid. Our view was, "Let's start paying it anyway, because it isn't a whole lot. It's very annoying, because it means another burden on us, but let's start paying it, be a good corporate citizen and have another look at it in six months' time." I think we thought we could then go in to the authorities and say, "You asked us to pay this tax. We've paid it. We are good citizens. When you ask us to do something we do it, but in the meantime will you tell us where this is going? We haven't budgeted for it. We're not sure whether it shouldn't be national treatment. What is Beijing's view on this?" We haven't done that to date, because we feel that that particular one is so far out of left field. If it had been an additional tax on something very local we would probably have gone in there and scrapped a bit. With that one we feel a little bit wary, as the local government is levying what is clearly a national tax.

'Why they have done that remains a mystery to us. We have assumed that this one might just go away. It was only levied on some enterprises. It wasn't levied across all joint ventures in Shanghai. We were also mystified about why *we* were asked to pay and others weren't. A lot of things are done in China on the quota system. The best example is the "strike hard" campaign against crime. Districts and localities within cities are given a quota of people to line up. It's a national thing. The word goes out that 2000 people are to be executed in the next few months and your quota is five. Your city's quota is 100. It goes out to the districts. The general managers of hotels are given a quota of pimps and prostitutes to arrest. You are given five before Chinese New Year and you have to find them. At the end of the week the quota is filled.'

Comment

Although the extra taxes are not crippling, they do demonstrate a view of a business entity as an organisation through which the government can carry out social and economic action. This was so during the communist period when society was assembled into work units, collectives and communes. However, administration through intermediate bodies goes back well beyond the communist period. The pattern before 1949 was for government officials to administer in collaboration with the local wealthy gentry clans, and in the towns and cities, with the commercial guilds.

On behalf of the government the gentry clans collected taxes, organised local defence, and funded and managed public works: irrigation systems, roads, bridges, dykes, dams, ferries, dredging and granaries. Gentry also established and managed relief works in times of famine, as well as orphanages, charity organisations, public cemeteries and private colleges. These areas were not considered the strict preserve of government responsibilities. At times the gentry also came into conflict with government officials when government actions threatened their interests—not unlike contemporary foreign businesses and the local bureaus (Chang 1955).

Since the introduction of the economic reforms in 1978, local officials have forced private Chinese businesses to pay ad hoc contributions to local infrastructure developments such as city appearance, traffic regulation and sanitation. And in order to get the co-operation of local officials, successful entrepreneurs have funded schools and tree-planting, provided jobs and free goods and services to poor families, and trained apprentices (Young 1995). Their 'voluntary donations' have funded roads and bridges, water and electricity supply, sewerage and drainage systems, parks and recreation areas, and new office buildings for township and district governments (Liu 1992). One researcher has described similar commercial 'contributions' (*juan*) or 'subscriptions' (*juanshu*)

made during the nineteenth century as 'a primitive form
of progressive income tax' (Rowe 1984, p. 195). Even
today this may in fact be the role of such exactions,
since it is well known that Chinese businesses often
do not pay tax or pay inadequate tax, some burning
their books at the end of each year to avoid official
scrutiny.

Chinese officials expect joint ventures to fund social
security, retirement, medical and housing programs. Some
foreign companies have found the only way to reduce the
workforce is to pay them benefits to stay at home. In
one case in Tianjin the foreign company pays 2 million
RMB a year to 200 people excess to their staffing needs.

In the case study of the relocation tax for returned
servicemen, the manager suspected that the local authorities were administering a national tax. This follows the
customary practice of the central authorities requesting
provincial authorities to administer special taxes to fund
military operations, military infrastructure and famine
relief in other parts of China (Rowe 1984, pp. 202–3).
For example, from Ming times (1368–1644) to Republi-
can times (1911–49), Fujian and Guangdong provinces
were taxed to pay for campaigns against Japanese pirates
(Mann 1987, p. 36).

Western enterprises expect to concern themselves
with business issues exclusively and, through clearly artic-
ulated and universally applied taxation systems, to
contribute to what government then takes responsibility
for organising: health, education, and a range of social
services and infrastructure development. But in China,
business entities have an extended role. Demands are
placed on them by government to contribute to specific
needs: the returned servicemen's relocation fund; blood
bank contributions; and infrastructure such as housing,
or the roads leading to the factory.

In the following case study a manager from Shanghai
discusses his reaction to the Chinese view that non-
government organisations are taxable entities for social
and charitable purposes.

Case study: Blood donations

'There are things which pop up from the government and take some understanding. There's the forced blood donation which was imposed in 1996. A foreign government donated a blood bank to Shanghai, but the Chinese didn't want to give blood. To ensure that the blood bank had sufficient supplies, the authorities decided to impose targets for donations. Since we are one of the bigger enterprises we were given a target of 26 people every six months. I found that unpleasant to swallow. We had to tell our workers, "You'll go. You'll give blood". I said, "Should the enterprise be doing this? It's *your* blood—it should be a voluntary thing". But the government thought otherwise. So we had to encourage them to go by drawing lots. Foreigners' blood wasn't accepted, so we were excluded.

'I let the Party educate the workforce about it. Lots of people said, "I'm sick that day", or "I'm taking one month's leave". But they gave them an allowance of seven days' leave for giving 500 millilitres of blood and a cash allowance of 700 RMB.

'From the company's point of view we were losing 26 people for a week, plus some money. We asked them, "How did you arrive at this decision? It's not good for our company. Plus the employees are upset, plus we have to spend time managing it." We still do it every six months. We ask other joint ventures around town if they have to give blood. They don't. So it depends on who the government chooses, and we are a large enterprise and therefore a target. The government says, "We are just doing our job. You can delay, you can pay us a fee not to do it. But we'll be back in six months' time." It was too hard to negotiate out of. Someone on high had said, "This is how it has to be". They had to fill the blood bank.'

16

Exorbitant levies and sundry taxes

The most colourful, although not the most appreciated, aspect of bureaucratic relations with business in China is that surrounding the taxing and regulation of business by local bureaucrats. Since bureaucrats have the power to interpret and implement central laws and regulations, and to devise and impose their own local regulations, individual bureaucrats take on great significance for business. A Chinese commentator put it this way: 'Official help is so important that most Chinese take it as a test of their friendship with others' (Zhu 1996).

The jurisdiction of local bureaus overlaps and their regulations sometimes conflict. Apparently this conflict does not worry the Chinese as much as it does Western managers. It is the Chinese view that conflict between regulations is to be expected: '[D]ifferences among local regulations and departmental rules or between local and departmental rules shall be considered as normal phenomena, and the existence of one regulation shall not negate or replace another regulation.' (Corne 1997, p. 147, quoting Ying and Dong 1991)

The next case study demonstrates the view and strategies of a Western general manager faced with this problem.

Case study: sixty different government departments

'The government environment has a lot of grey areas. People in the government who think they have jurisdiction over you really don't, but they will try and say they do. We come under the Shanghai government. Then we have local bureaus also coming along to assist us. They come to inspect the hygiene. We say, "But the Shanghai government does that. Why are we having you do it?" They reply, "Because we are responsible". We say, "But we had them last week, and now you are coming this week. OK, fine. Do your inspection". They want to be involved in an enterprise that is growing and that is important in the district. They want to have a look. And there are a lot of government agencies, something like 60. At any time they can come and pay a visit to see how things are going and talk about whatever issues they want to talk about.

'We have people who look after them and talk to them. If we want something from them, then we have the relationship and we know where to go. The expatriate in charge of the factory handles the production-related relationships. From time to time they come along and test our waste water to see what chemical elements are in it, and to see whether the pipes are being treated properly. He will receive them, talk to them for a while, see what they want, escort them around the factory, invite them to lunch, talk about whatever they want to talk about.

'Quite often it's related to money. Everything is open to negotiation, so you discuss it and hope the person can get them to a level that is acceptable. They expect that. They come along and say,

"We think that for this you should pay a certificate fee of . . . '. And we say, "Oh, we think that's a bit high". Often we just give them a drink and lunch and they are happy.

'We had the Occupational Health and Safety come through. They fined us 10 000 RMB. The local Light Industry Bureau, who are our partners, took them out to a banquet and got it down to 1000 RMB. This is happening a lot. We are a target. All these bureaus have come through in the last few months. They do a general audit. They say, "You haven't been checking your measuring equipment enough. We're going to fine you 20 000 RMB". So our Chinese partner takes them out for dinner and we give them 2000 RMB.

'I guess that in our home environment the charges would be regular and set in black and white, and probably higher. The charges here are imposed more often, but are lower, and are open to negotiation or delay, or some other way of dealing with it. All this negotiating and discussing is very time consuming. They have so many people in the government looking for revenue-generating activities to support housing or some other project.

'It is always a case of having to sit down with the authorities and negotiate your way through these things, because they can make life extremely difficult for you. Foreign investors have to have a fairly practical approach to these problems. Rather than fight city hall, you are better advised to sit down with the people involved and work through the issues. Often it's easier to make a cash contribution. Obviously one tries to negotiate down as far as possible and dispose of the issue, retain your relationship with the local authorities and continue production.'

Comment

In the 1980s over 50 per cent of the state budget was devolved to the provinces. Tax collection was placed in the hands of local governments. They shared the revenues upwards according to individually negotiated agreements. Tax and revenue-sharing systems are not governed by uniform rules established by law and enforced by the courts. There are many complexities, with different treatment given to different enterprises depending on their ownership. Local enterprises are able to negotiate special tax reductions with their governing bureaus.

Budgets at the local level are tight because of a decline in their share of GNP, forced subsidies imposed by the central government and a significant expansion in local government administration (Wong et al. 1995).

The method companies use to deal with the exactions of local bureaus is important. In the case study, the company executives adopted a flexible and creative method with an emphasis on negotiation. They were also quite 'Chinese' in using lunches and banquets as an influence strategy. Another company tried a different approach in dealing with the endless bureau inspections and fines; they ran the bureau officials off the premises. A short while later the bureau concerned imposed a complete audit on the company's financial accounts with which it had to comply.

Tax, a fundamental instrument of government, is 'an area in which discretionary treatment is entrenched . . . especially in the granting of exemptions and privileges or the authorising of alternative methods of computing profits and depreciation of fixed assets' (Corne 1997, p. 101).

Case study: The tax bureaus

'Tax is an area where a foreign-owned joint venture, particularly if it is understood that it is a fairly large company from overseas, has lots of money, and we, the tax department, want a piece of it. We'll have the sales tax people in one week, the payroll people the next week. We'll have the tax department that's in charge of ensuring that any scrap that is sold goes to licensed scrap dealers in the next week to check our scrap records—and that's just at the city level. Then at some stage you get the provincial people coming in to do the same kind of checks. It ties up your administrative staff and management staff with this inordinate number of audits.

'We have talked to them about this. They are always prepared to negotiate on the fine, and there is always a fine. It's criminal. Someone has said, "The Chinese play by the rules—the only trouble is that there are lots of rules to choose from". Everything is negotiable. They have the ability to unilaterally impose something on a business, retrospectively, and you have no right of redress. You can't deal with that. The tax department decides that a tax should be imposed on you back here, but there's no statute, there's no decree or anything. They just decide that you are liable for it. You can object. But who do you object to? There is no higher authority. If you don't want to pay it, you get charged. And if you don't pay, the directors go to gaol. It is a totalitarian situation which they dress up to look legitimate. It's anything but. So there is that sort of relationship with the bureaucrats. It's on-going and relatively petty. It's more of a nuisance than a real impediment to business. Every now and again you get a claim for US$200 000. You end up settling it for $4333. The tax official gets $2000 in his pocket, and it costs you another $2333 as assessed. That's on-going.'

Comment

From the time of the Song dynasty (960–1279) the phenomenon of 'local tax bullies' has been documented. The central government farmed out taxation collection to local-level officials and non-bureaucratic organisations, who would set up private tax stations. Rapacious officials thus had the opportunity to collect illegal fees and surcharges.

In 1160 a report described the excesses of the taxation system thus: 'Boats plying the waterways may be detained for a fortnight while they are assessed for taxes; in the worst cases, the crews' own food and clothing are taxed as if they were goods for commercial sale.' (Mann 1987, p. 33)

A traveller in the 1890s, T.T. Cooper, was approached by Chinese merchants to join them in setting up an insurance company. They would contribute the capital if he would agree to use his own name 'in order to secure it from the depredations of the Mandarins, who they said would not dare squeeze a foreigner'. This, of course, was in the days when gunboats and colonial power provided a certain level of protection (Cooper 1871).

Cases of local officials applying what used to be called 'the squeeze' for their own purposes are commonly reported. In the mid-nineteenth century the central government had to issue an edict forbidding officials from issuing extra licences 'on their own authority'. Local officials were known to increase the cost of brokerage licences mandated by the government at between one half and two taels to 25 or even 55 taels (Mann 1987, pp. 44–46). This practice continues and the central government has ordered local officials to abandon the practice.

While many Westerners feel that fines and taxes are primarily directed against foreign-invested enterprises, in fact, Chinese small business people suffer from 'discretionary implementation' just as much as Western business in China. The following account gives a rare insight into the relations between tax bureaus and Chinese small business.

Chinese small businesses and the tax bureaus

In a study of the business life of private households in Chengdu, in Sichuan province, between 1987 and 1991, small-scale local business people generally regarded the bureaucracy as an obstacle to the expansion of business and profit-making. They had a saying, 'bureaucrats shielding one another' (*guanguan xianghu*). Most business people believed that 'the bigger your business, the more officials you are visited by' (Bruun 1993, p. 120).

During the three years of this study of the business situation in Chengdu, local supplementary fees increased 100–200 per cent, and the number of bureaus collecting them doubled, from five to ten. Some of the new charges were:

- a security charge issued by the local police station;
- a culture charge, issued by the municipal culture bureau;
- an education charge issued by the bureau of education;
- a city reconstruction charge issued by the Chengdu Bureau of City Reconstruction; and
- a temporary residence charge issued to all employees and paid to the street committee.

The head of the local police station had a particularly bad reputation. He used many officials and petty officials (volunteers from the street committee and other low-level organisations) to collect large sums of money from businesses in his district as 'security charges'.

This ability of the officials to build empires for themselves and to exercise power irrespective of central policies was frequently commented on by local business people. Sayings about the officials, called the 'uncrowned kings', are numerous: 'when the gods fight, the people

suffer' and 'the officials burn houses while commoners
are not permitted to burn oil lamps'.

Small-time entrepreneurs needing licences to start up
new businesses were faced with demands from officials
in a range of bureaus for large sums of money. The
process of gaining licences involved long periods of 'pend-
ing' when the parties would try out each other—the
applicant offering increasing amounts of cigarettes, liquor
and cash payments without knowing the effect, and the
official playing with the upper limits of the applicant's
capacity. Some individuals were prevented from gaining
a licence, although they had the money.

It was local opinion that charges are determined at
will by the local bureaus. Although tax is a central
government matter, it was as unregulated as the local
charges. In an effort to regularise the tax charges, the
central government had demanded book-keeping by businesses in 1987, 1988 and 1989. So, in 1988 all local
businesses in Chengdu were told to keep account books.
This they did. But when it was time to collect the tax,
their figures were rejected even as a basis for negotiation.
According to Bruun, 'tax is . . . collected according to
the responsible official's intuitive assessment of the "true
figure"'.

The tax bureau was considered the most corrupt of
all bureaus by the local people. They had no access to
how the amount they paid was reached. This was decided
by tax officials, and collected by petty officials belonging
to the Self-Employed Labourers' Association.

Because of the impenetrable nature of the tax calcu-
lations, the tax paid by individual businesses could be
adjusted through relationships. As Bruun found, 'Tax
evasion proved to be out of the question for some,
possible for others, and a matter of course for a few of
the wealthiest households and those with direct connection to the bureau via Association work'. A Mrs Luo who
operated a grocery shop was of the opinion that '[i]f you
. . . show off your wealth, like wearing expensive clothes
or watches, they charge you more'.

Bruun met one of the tax collectors in the free market. He found that tax was not only based on turn-over, but on 'co-operativeness'. She told him, ' . . . if any of them carry out illegal trade we charge them extra. If . . . they pump up chickens with water or sell products of inferior quality—in these cases tax can be as high as 30 per cent, depending on their political attitude, their agreement with government policies, and their attitude toward us'.

It was common that even after tax had been paid, an extra tax charge would be levied at the end of the year. This amounted to several hundred yuan, and the reason for it would not be known to the business people levied.

From his study of the interaction between small private businesses and the local authorities, Bruun con-cluded that 'contradictions between the policies of the central government and local interpretations were inherent to the system', a conclusion that is no news for Western managers.

Strategies

In dealing with this apparently uncontrolled exercise of bureaucratic power, local people used the concept of 'fair treatment' (*zhengdang*) rather than any appeal to law and legality. The head of the Industrial and Commercial Administration Bureau (Gong Shang Ju), which repre-sented the Ministry of Industry and Commerce, was questioned by Bruun. The bureau is responsible for small business and issues permits, registration, supervision and advice on management. In reply to a question on the legality of extra charges the bureau head replied, 'I don't think it is a question of whether they are legal, but if they are reasonable'—an interesting negotiating point for Western executives.

17

Mutual co-operation, mutual benefits

A successful Chinese restaurant owner had a strategy for dealing with the regulatory bureaucrats. It was to '*yan jiu, yan jiu*'. '*Yan jiu*' means 'to study' or to 'give thought to something'. But by altering the tone on each character he meant 'cigarettes and liquor': a different type of 'study' (Bruun 1993).

In this unstable, personalised policy climate where the state has greater power than the members of society, Chinese entrepreneurs protect their business interests by linking themselves to local bureaucrats in patron–client ties. Chinese entrepreneurs in Xiamen city referred to their patrons in the bureaucracy as 'backstage bosses' (*houtai laoban*) and 'supporters' (*kaoshan*) (Wank 1996).

Another strategy used by Chinese entrepreneurs for dealing with bureaucrats is to 'wear the red hat'. Entrepreneurs disguise the private nature of their firms by organising a collective enterprise with the neighbourhood committee and paying them a management fee. This ensures them of protection from the state. As a result in Wenzhou, where research was carried out, only ten of 10 000 businesses that were really private firms registered as such. The others 'wore the red hat' (Parris 1993).

Local cadres shelter these so-called collective businesses from state interference because they benefit, both personally and collectively, from the income they generate. Local Wenzhou officials owned 2000 of 7000 new apartment buildings that had been constructed with private funds. A further one-quarter of the four-storey apartment buildings in a nearby commercial township were owned by officials (Liu 1992).

In return for benefits from the profits and skills of private business, bureaucrats provide access to information about policy thinking in the government and the likely interpretation of the policy at the local level, access to licences, facilitation in administrative procedures and access to raw materials, public sector markets and infrastructure. They can also impose local protectionism by setting up 'inspection stations' on their borders to block the entry of competitive products into their area (Nee 1992). Provincial authorities also protect foreign industries by giving preferential treatment to foreign partners and erecting tariff barriers against foreign companies located in other areas. This is particularly evident in the automobile industry. Any company associated with Shanghai Volkswagen is excluded from supplying parts to the automotive industries in north and south China.

In the West, the legal system is the foundation upon which trust in commercial relationships is built. This provides certainty, so that you know what is expected; equality, so that the same standard is applied to all in the same circumstances; and legislative purpose according to which all implementing agencies demonstrate common goals (Corne 1997, p. 100).

In China, trust in commercial relationships is not built on a legal foundation but through specific ties to individuals. Such ties are not transferable to others. From mutual co-operation come mutual benefits. Those government impositions that Western companies complain about, what the Chinese call 'exorbitant levies and sundry taxes' (*kejuan zashui*), are dealt with by Chinese business entrepreneurs through personal ties and sharing financial benefits. This list of 'benefits' shared with officials, which would be regarded as corruption in the

West, comes from entrepreneurs in Xiamen city in Fujian province:

- Providing a 50 per cent commission to friends in the bureaucracy who can travel in China at the public expense and open sales outlets inter-regionally.
- Providing retaining fees to 'advisers', non-transferable company shares, positions on the board of directors, welfare benefits such as medical and retirement supplements.
- Providing gifts, such as bottles of wine and spirits, television sets, or red envelopes stuffed with cash to pay for children's education. Gifts have a special place in forging ties and are generally expected to produce loyalty in the recipient in a way not understood in the West.
- Sharing advantages, such as giving officials a lift in a chauffeured car to other cities, thus saving them the unpleasantness of overcrowded public transport.
- Wining and dining officials in sumptuous restaurants owned by the business group.
- Giving discounts on functions. For example, 'One official had his daughter's wedding party in an entre-preneur's ornate restaurant, which gave him a double obligation as he received a steep price discount as well as face by the party's lavish setting' (Wank 1996, p. 835).

Hierarchy of relationships

However, there is a subtlety to patronage ties with offi-cials. It is not simply a matter of benefits. This makes it easier to see how foreign firms could find China a hostile environment if they are without the right connec-tions. According to the Chinese entrepreneurs of Xiamen, ties based solely on commercial considerations are the weakest. These are known as 'money ties' (*jinqian*) or 'self-interest ties' (*liyi*). The strongest and most produc-tive are *tianzi* ties—those produced by birth. Workers in the bureaucracy, in the commercial bureaus, foreign trade and tax bureaus, or in the People's Liberation Army which staffs transportation, harbour management and public security in the city government, have many ways of helping relatives who have gone out into private business. This brings to mind the relationship between official and gentry in imperial times: some members of the gentry staffed the imperial bureaucracy, and other members made money from land-owning and commercial activities, such as pawn-broking or running government monopolies such as the salt gabelle. And purely commercial families, when they had the opportunity, would buy degrees and official brevets to give them entry to official circles.

Following closely on blood relationships are those relationships formed prior to the entrepreneur's business career that involve emotional attachments with people (*ganqing*), such as classmates, colleagues with whom they worked in the state-owned enterprises, and government ministries and bureaus of the socialist period. In the 1988 economic rectification campaign in Xiamen, it was entrepreneurs with only 'money ties' to patrons who suffered most from investigations and arrests. Those who had patrons based on kinship ties and 'emotional attachments' were largely spared the crackdown.

Another path for entrepreneurs to develop patron–client ties is by taking on quasi-official roles in business associations, such as the Individual Labourers' Association and the Young Factory Director and Management Association. These organisations are sponsored by the Industry and Commerce Bureau. Office-holders have access to the bureaus that have discretionary power over private business.

It is difficult for foreign businesses to handle their relationships with officials as the locals do, because most foreign businesses are structured public companies with boards of directors who report to shareholders and to their own country's monitoring authorities. Many Chinese-style business relationships would contravene corporate governance requirements. Other means need to be devised.

In the following case studies, the interesting point is the strategies adopted by Western managers to gain the co-operation of the bureaucrats.

Case study: Solid gold scissors

'We got to know a lot of the local officials by starting a small assembly factory. It didn't cost us much at all. The big gain was spending several years just understanding how the local system works, who the players were and who we had to know for the next step, which is buying land and building a factory.

'It's a state-run economy, so everything is owned and run by the government. But at the municipal level, there might be 20 million people under the control of the local mayor—he's like God. He is nominated by the Party, and he basically decides everything. There are mayors of villages, and they have rights and control over land. If they want to raise money they'll say, "We will hive off this land for an industrial estate". They usually do a deal with one of the municipal corporations—the Foreign Trade and Investment Co-operation Corporation, say. They will have a director, a Party man and about three vice directors who are now usually switched-on, smart, business-oriented people who know what a dollar is all about.

'The local mayor, who doesn't know a lot about it, tends to use the government corporations to help him to develop the local site and to help sell it off. In our case the deputy director of one of the corporations was also the director of another municipal corporation called the Foreign Investment Co-operation Committee which approves all imports. The structure bears no relationship to anything you can call logic. Ever. You have the most illogical groups of corporations, all cross-linked, that you never see in the West.

'I was very insistent that we have a wholly foreign-owned enterprise. Most foreign companies give 10–20 per cent equity to the Chinese, so that their partner understands and does all the dealing with the government. But you've got the problem that the 20 per cent wants to own the manager. Even with a wholly-owned enterprise, you need the co-operation of government, you need the co-operation of all these officials to get things done. If you don't have these local petty government officials on side, they can make your life a nightmare. They won't do things like give you approvals, for, say, waste water disposal.

'The biggest thing to be concerned about is when the local government says there will be power or water to your site. There may be firm dates written into the contract, but the chances of it happening are pretty remote. You've got to watch like a hawk through the building program and take action yourself, otherwise your plant might sit there for a year without being able to run: you could have US$20 million in investment unable to run.

'To start up a factory you need maybe 140 "chops"—the little official stamps put on documents to show approval. If you miss out on one, you can't run your operation. You're stopped. Health, safety, fire, water connection, waste water and sewerage, telephone lines, footpaths . . . it just goes on and on and on . . . all different departments. We held a big banquet in Hong Kong and got them all to chop the approvals as they left.

'To be able to deal with the myriad of government departments we negotiated with the
co-operation committee that we would have a
contract of fee-for-service. The committee's role
was to assist companies get established in that area
with a minimum of government interference. And
all of a sudden here was this company that comes
along and says, "We just want you to do what you
normally do, but we want to sign a contract with
you that, as we do better, we'll keep paying you
money".'

Relationship building

'Every time I went to China I made a big point
of lining up the local mayor and the directors of
the committee for a banquet. When the board
goes to visit, we go up the river by ferry. The local
mayor sends his chauffeur-driven SEL Mercedes to
meet us at his expense, to drive our directors to
the factory and back. When I took the company
board to China for the opening, the local mayor
organised a police escort from the ferry even
though it was out of his municipal area. All the
traffic lights went on green and we had a police
motorcycle escort—it was about one-and-a-half
hours to our factory. They weren't allowed to put
on their sirens and lights until we entered their
municipal area. He put all that on at a cost. They
came and had a look at the factory a couple of
days before we opened it. They said we could do
with some more flowers. That afternoon two
trucks arrived and there were cane baskets absolutely full of flowers.

'At the opening of the factory we had lunch,
then we had five people cut the ribbon to open
the factory, and I made sure that a couple of them

were local bureaucrats. I really tried to make them part of the deal, although they had not one cent in the business. At the cutting of the ribbon, the mayor was given a pair of solid gold scissors as his memento of the deal. It's horses for courses.

'The bureaucracy is a movable feast. People get moved around in the departments. You've got to work out on a day-to-day basis who is important to what. I was getting along very well with the previous mayor when all of a sudden, pht! gone! Overnight. He got side-stepped into some relatively minor role. They brought in a man from Shanghai. He's the mayor of this huge area in southern China, and I suspect because the power-brokers in Beijing are all from Shanghai, they are loyal henchmen of the power-brokers in Beijing. He's short, he's surrounded by people, and he drives around in this great big black 600 SEL Mercedes. He basically rules a big chunk of southern China.

'I wanted to take a whole lot of good wine to the opening. Through the co-operation committee and the local mayor, they brought in all the wine from Hong Kong in the boot of the Mercedes in about three trips. No duty.'

Comment

Unlike so many companies who went into China—and still go into China—without understanding the local system, this company spent a number of years operating at low cost in the area they were considering as a major investment site. They got to learn about the power-holders and the links between different parts of the bureaucracy and about what mattered to them. That is why they proposed to the Foreign Trade and Investment

Co-operation Committee that they would earn a percentage on the company's smooth operation. Although the fee-for-service meant very little in monetary terms to the foreign company, what they received in return—efficiency in gaining the chops on their approval forms and the expediting of on-going approvals—was worth a great deal. They have actually borrowed from the strategies of Chinese entrepreneurs and are 'wearing the red hat', foreign-style.

The foreign investment was important to the mayor of the local area, and he was able to facilitate approvals involved in the purchase of the land and the building of the factory. Within his own district he had power. However, just because a business has links with the bureaucracy doesn't make for preferential treatment. That is why knowing the actual local situation is so important. The executive quoted in Chapter 6 whose business was located in Shanghai found that their links into high levels of the bureaucracy only meant 'a weekly meeting with a whole bunch of bureaucrats who don't contribute anything'. The executive involved in that venture advised other investors to come in 'under the radar' and not to seek high-profile recognition, and certainly not to allow the board to be dominated by Chinese directors.

This case study executive decided on a wholly-owned enterprise after observing the outcomes for foreign joint ventures. Instead of gaining local co-operation and local knowledge by the joint venture structure, he gained co-operation by his purely commercial tactic of fee-for-service. He thus avoided the difficult experience of sharing joint venture management, and the equally difficult and unpleasant process of buying out the joint venture partner.

Companies who have moved from a joint venture structure to wholly-owned have found other ways than through a joint venture to gain the co-operation of bureau officials, such as employing Chinese people with standing—an ex-mayor, say, or people who formerly worked in the Ministry of Foreign Trade and Economic

Co-operation, or the tax or customs bureaus, and who have kept up those relationships.

The executive makes the point that relations with the bureaucracy need to be worked on continuously as people and regulations change. Even Chinese companies don't always know the relevent bureaucrats. Some companies with operations in different parts of China use their knowledge of local requirements and relationships with the bureaucracy to get approvals for their overall business. For example, in Shanghai the bureaucracies follow the rules very closely and require a lot of documentation before approvals are given. But in other places, such as in south China, they might only require half of what Shanghai requires, and there might be someone 'willing to bend forward a little'. So that is where they will direct their approval effort.

Gestures like giving the mayor a pair of gold scissors as a memento of the opening of a new factory are important in the hierarchical nature of Chinese administration. As the Western manager said, 'Horses for courses'. These sorts of symbolic gestures emphasise status while avoiding the dangers of corruption.

18

Talking to the bureaucrats

'Risk-averse' is a common description given by Western business people to Chinese bureaucrats. Risk-averse behaviour results in decisions being postponed or passed up the hierarchy. Communication from the bureaucracy to business is not always very good. Matters not relevant to a particular department can be put aside and forgotten, and you may not be told that this is what has happened. Proactive action is necessary to progress matters through the bureaucracy. Bureaucrats make their decisions based on rule books. So when Western companies approach with a different way of doing something, the Chinese bureaucrat is faced with a problem: it is not according to the rule books, so he becomes responsible if the proposed matter goes wrong. Chinese administrators also have to balance the sensitivities of different departments because jurisdictions overlap. Such complexities are usually hidden from Western business people.

Westerners must understand the process, who is behind the process, who has the authority and the chops to keep the matter moving. There are few published regulations available to the public. This forces people back on to relationships to find out how to expedite matters. Here is what an executive in a multinational manufacturing company based in Shanghai learned.

Case study: Finding the right door

'Part of the joint venture agreement was that our partner would organise the approvals for the expansion of our factory so that we could double our output. It was all written down, but nothing happened. It was just delayed and delayed and delayed. So, through various means I got to meet the person who was holding the application. She just said, "You've got the wrong door". Our partner, a Chinese company, didn't know which door to go through. So, rather than reject the application and send it back, she just let it sit on her desk and said to herself, "It's not my responsibility". That's how we found out that we are now part of the administrative responsibility of the Shanghai government, rather than of the district we are located in, and that we should go to them for approvals. She was very happy to introduce us to the Shanghai government person responsible. Within a week it was fixed. So, not only did *we* need to learn how to do business, but our partner who had been doing business in Shanghai for 40 years hadn't known which way to go.

'You have to learn to find the ways through. All departments present their own problems. You have to learn how to get around them: whether it's relieving them of having to make a decision by almost making the decision for them, or implying it has already been decided, and then taking them out to lunch. Relationships in the approval processes are just as important as relationships in the business deal. You can't be heavy-handed. You can't use stand-over negotiating. It doesn't work. They'll just procrastinate forever. It's no skin off their nose if the factory is a year late, because they didn't approve it.'

Relationships and responsibility

'You can get into a hell of a log-jam, so you have to keep up the relationships. Many things depend on the interpretation. It's knowing who has the authority to interpret the rules and what moti- vates them. How do you remove them from a traceable responsibility? For a bureaucratic de- partment head you find a way so that the responsibility for a decision doesn't end up on his shoulders. You learn this because it takes so long to get something done.

'An example of this process was getting our gas approvals. The person who had to sign off was going to have responsibility for the safety of that plant and he couldn't handle it. So we had to work our way through the design department to get them to sign off that this was a safe design, before he would sign that it was now an approved design for that site. The safety issue had been removed from him, and he could always blame the engineers. We took the engineers to lunch and talked to them about international safety stand- ards. They thought the standards were great and that it was very helpful. The proof we gave him about those standards was his escape. If something went wrong, he would find a way to say that it was not his fault, that he did it on designs approved by someone else.

'We talk a lot to them to find out what the department structure is and who has the authority. You go and see more and more people, see other companies and find out who chops their approvals. It's a lot of hard work. Departments tell you to come back another time. You have to be very persistent. Sometimes I would sit in their office until they agreed to do something. One tactic they used was to change appointments.

'One department absolutely insisted that everything on site had to be inspected in the containers before they were released. It was just impossible to get someone to go and do that, in terms of timeliness, so we went ahead and got them out anyway. We had been nursing that department along, and finally we took the fellow out, bought him a dinner and it was fine. They had the authority to *not* sign the paper that entitled us to get an operating licence.

'Now we are working to get our product stamped as an environmentally friendly product. We've described our product according to Chinese environmental standards. The Chinese produce books of approved products and processes. We want to get our products in those books. So, we have to work with various ministries to get our products endorsed. We are working on the bureaucracies all the time. It's a huge amount of work.'

Comment

What Western managers find different from their dealings with the bureaucracy at home is the lack of a helpful attitude. Information isn't freely given unless they have good personal relationships. The Chinese bureaucracy is personalised as opposed to impersonal. Because a Westerner is not familiar with the rules means that there are hold-ups. He or she may not have accurately and meticulously completed documents. Chinese government departments have an abundance of workers to check all forms thoroughly. This, coupled with the national preference for attention to detail, ensures that discrepancies in documentation will be spotted, bringing the process to a halt. Even a stamp crossing a line on the document can result in non-approval. To find out where the difficulty lies, Western managers have to talk to the responsible officers. This is more easily said than done. The matter may cross the jurisdiction of a number of departments, and it may not be easy to track down which departments are involved and who in those departments is the responsible person. Chinese bureaucracies are staffed with large numbers of functionaries. People lower in the echelon dare not make decisions that are the preserve of their bosses. It is necessary to track the chain of command to reach the person who makes the decision.

In the construction industry, as in many other industries, the Chinese want to use their own research and design institutes. The next case study comes from a multinational construction company with projects in different parts of China. It describes how a Western executive dealt with the design institutes and the general bureaucratic process.

Case study: Equals and friends

'When our first container came through we had to go to the Shanghai docks and talk to the authorities there. Until they got to know us, we didn't exist. Their attitude towards regulations is, "I won't provide any assistance because it gets me into trouble". Until we understood that better, we struggled. Whereas if you go to the docks in Melbourne, the union guy will say, "Oh, you're wasting your time, mate" and will give you some suggestions. We were newcomers trying to find one container. The Shanghai container storage is enormous. Our problem was that we didn't know the system. I don't think they are being vindictive; it's just our lack of knowledge of how they work.

'In dealing with the bureaucracy you can't expect a Western response. A Western response might be a five-minute response to give you the answer you want. In China you get frustrated after the third week, and you eventually find that you could have done it three weeks ago. When we first went to Suzhou it took us seven weeks to open a bank account. We were frustrated that things were going wrong. It took us only two weeks in Tianjin. The reason was, we knew the ropes. We thought they were being difficult, but we didn't have all the permits and all the regulations in place.

'People go there with the wrong attitude. They don't acknowledge that it's a different system and they have to know and understand the system. They start applying Western standards, and when they don't achieve what they want, they can get very dogmatic. Because everything is so slow, some of them start saying, "Well, how can I speed this up? How much money do you want?"

'In Suzhou, after we'd been there for six months, we discovered that we didn't have the right cards to work there. They came on-site and said, "You don't have the right cards". We said, "But we've got all the stamps and all the author-isations". But there was a separate card—there are green cards and brown cards—and we didn't have one of these cards. We said, "But how is it possible that we've been working here for six months with the wrong cards?" They said, "Oh, the regulations have changed", or "There is a new man". Either they were just covering up as they had made a mistake, or there genuinely was a change. So we asked them to show us the forms. They did that, and we filled in the forms—it was OK.'

The design institutes

'To get approval to build, the Chinese design institutes have to chop the drawing to indicate that it is their drawing. They are then responsible for getting the approvals from the various authorities. They have a preliminary approval presentation where the concept is presented to all the authorities. It can be up to 22 authorities. The design institute has usually informed them beforehand about the project. They all come together at a single meeting to discuss the plan, and give preliminary approval. They do it in great depth, highly technically-oriented, and very high and strict on environmental stuff, especially with Westerners, in regard to fire regulations and earthquakes.

'If you go to the design institute with a proposal, it's quite possible that they will say, "Sorry, it's impossible to do". They are so used to doing things according to a code. For instance, the regulations about protecting steel in a building. They want it protected by concrete. When you go round to the fire authority and discuss with them the relevant regulations and how they apply, you'll find that there is another way of protecting steel that might be with a spray, and that might be a better way of doing things. The fire authority man will then make a decision that it is OK, so he'll chop the drawings. But you don't ever get total approval. You get permission to build, but then when you've finished building you've got to get all these guys to come and have a look and chop the drawings again.

'Some of them will say, "Sorry, I want this, this and this". You say, "You've given us an approval and you said it was alright, and this is what we've done". And they'll say, "Well, it's not according to the regulation". So you've got to go right through the whole thing again. Sometimes with the same person, sometimes with a different person. That's why you have to establish this good relationship with the authorities, so they are talking to you as equals and as friends trying to reach a logical conclusion which is going to satisfy both the authorities and your own situation.'

Introductions to a bureaucrat

'We wanted to get the forms and make an appointment with the person in charge of registrations. I made the mistake of sending a woman interpreter to him to get the forms and make the appointment. He kicked her out of his office. He wouldn't talk to her. He said, "Mr Dixon has to come and see me himself". I wrote and apologised, and the next time I was in Tianjin, I asked to see this gentleman. He said, "I'm too busy". I said, "How about some time next week?" "I'm busy next week as well. I'm a very busy man."

'I quickly got the message: I was trying to approach him without an introduction. I then spent the next week trying to find a person who knew him. Eventually we unearthed somebody. Before the end of the week, that person asked me, "Can you meet him at eight o'clock on Thursday morning?" I said, "Of course I can. How did you manage that?" He replied, "Oh, he is a good friend of mine".

'When we met him, he was delightful. We exchanged presents. We talked about Australia, and not about the business at all. At the end he gave me the forms and asked me to come back when we'd filled them in. Whenever I phone him now, it's "Yes, come in and see me". We got off on the wrong foot because the interpreter took things into her own hands and went to another department instead of going only to this person. He went through the roof. He said, "Everything has to come through me".

'He was reasonably senior, officious, young, friendly, a bit shy, a bit overworked and frustrated by dealing with foreigners who don't know what they are talking about. All the Chinese said, "Oh, he is a very important man". He is a middle manager, efficient, well-respected. If you didn't get a permit from him it would be very difficult to go further up the chain. We would have to get the politicians involved. We didn't want to do that. When you try to do it the Western way there are all sorts of walls that build up. Do it the Chinese way. Give them the indication that you are willing to deal in the Chinese way.

'We've made it our business to get to know him very well, along with his boss and *his* boss. We are just one company of hundreds that are continually worrying these guys, companies who can't speak the language, don't know the system, want to be spoonfed with everything. If you understand *that*, you are probably able to deal with them better.

'You have to put the effort in yourself to "become Chinese" in your attitude, and you have to spend time on the ground making good relationships. You cannot employ a single Chinese person who knows how to get everything through the different authorities.'

Comment

This executive has provided some useful strategies in dealing with the bureaucracy:

- acknowledge differences in procedures;
- acknowledge that you are an outsider and unknown;
- acknowledge the risk-averse problem;
- realise that things are going to take time, but with experience they will speed up and go more smoothly;
- prepare for minute examination of technical details and documentation;
- talk around the regulations with different authorities;
- make a personal approach to people with status in the hierarchy; and
- recognise the frustration which non-Chinese-speaking foreigners cause for the Chinese.

A foreigner with a serious commercial problem relating to the bureaucracy put his case clearly to the vice mayor, and then to the departmental person handling the matter. He invited that person to the Hilton for coffee.

'It was a nice environment. It was quiet. We could talk through the problem without interruptions. I just explained to him how we view things in the West, and that it's not necessarily right, but I had to try and balance it for both sides. So I said to him, "If you undertake as a friend to go away and work through this, I will undertake to give as much help as I can from my side". I asked the departmental head to coffee a number of times to make sure that he realised how important the issue was for me and to keep tabs on how it was coming along. The more we talked, the greater our friendship and the more we talked about things other than the problem. In the end the problem was solved quietly, without any fuss, by people in the bureaucracy.'

This is yet another illustration of the importance of establishing a good relationship 'as equals and friends trying to reach a logical conclusion'. Since relationships mean so much to the Chinese as a way of facilitating business, Western executives would do well to take a positive approach and accept relationship-building as a major business strategy. Since there are said to be 10.8 million bureaucrats and they control so many essentials for business, their co-operation is worth fostering.

19

Conclusion

Running a successful business in China is an on-going challenge for Western managers. Assumptions held in the West cannot be automatically applied to China—the role of government in relation to business, global business conventions, manager–staff relationships, and ethical standards and their enforcement. Western managers have to know about the local, unwritten rules if they are to negotiate successful outcomes for their corporate policies and goals. This can often mean changing behaviour and learning new strategies.

A European manager in the United States, as long as he or she speaks English, can quickly assimilate into the local scene by joining the golf club, Rotary or Apex, or by attending business lunches and networking forums. In these networks he or she builds relationships and learns the unwritten rules of the local business community.

In China there is no such easy assimilation. There appears to be a large divide between a Western manager and the Chinese. Most Western managers exclude themselves from Chinese life. They live in apartments and villas that, by normal Chinese standards, are luxurious. They spend their leisure time with other foreigners. Their recreational interests are foreign. Their salaries are hundreds of times higher than local salaries—and the Chinese know it. Most are transients, sojourners, seen by the Chinese as only passing through. This makes the issue of trust in business relationships difficult to achieve— thus opening the way for the Chinese to treat foreign business people impersonally and to wring from them all the profit and benefit possible.

Westerners can feel excluded by the Chinese. Foreigners look so out of place among the Chinese, with their black hair and brown eyes. Chinese society consists of very large numbers of people living closely, working closely and who have a strong sense of 'Chineseness'. Any stranger who cannot speak the language of the local community is largely excluded from it, and the Chinese language, unrelated as it is to any Western language, presents a special barrier. Most Chinese have had little contact with Westerners. Western business people are easily identified as outsiders. They are under scrutiny from Chinese managers and employees. The locals will soon note their strengths and weaknesses and use them to advantage.

Despite these barriers there are many Westerners who fit well into the Chinese business scene. They find it stimulating, they get on well with Chinese people, they are successful and may stay for years. Even short-term sojourners can find niches for contact, such as through their wives teaching English in the local schools or some skill of their own which the Chinese value. My point here is not that China is an intolerably hostile environment for Westerners, but that the points of cultural difference cannot be lightly dismissed. This has been made clear in the case studies.

Some executives say that what they have experienced in China has made them better managers, better able to listen and to communicate, more flexible in their problem-solving. Others say that what they have learned is China-specific, with very little that is transferable to a wider global business context. Those China-specific pieces of knowledge are discussed below.

Chinese interests

The Chinese want to learn foreign skills, adopt foreign technology, make money and become powerful. At this point in their history, they have an attitude of commercial nationalism. They live in a strong, all-embracing culture, confident in its values. This can make for resistance to Western methods and Western goals.

Power-holders in the bureaucracy—the mayors, vice mayors, magistrates and bureau officials—are responsible for local economic well-being and social stability. This results in a strong tendency for them to favour Chinese businesses. Much of it happens secretly. In the tax area, local tax bureaus will exclude foreign accountancy firms by recommending to local and foreign businesses former government employees now running independent tax companies. They then provide these tax companies with confidential government information. No foreign company can ignore local power-holders and their interests.

The market has not been as welcoming as expected. Many Chinese prefer to buy Chinese goods, and their lower prices make them attractive. In joint ventures, Chinese partners are not always willing to share benefits and adopt capitalist thinking. Employees vary from young and inexperienced but keen to learn, to older employees too experienced in the old socialist work practices and with a dislike of foreigners.

Manager–subordinate relationships

A major undertaking for Western managers has been to transfer Western management and technical knowledge to Chinese staff. In some areas such as textile and garment manufacture the Chinese already had skills and expertise, and quickly adapted to the new technology. But in most cases, Western executives did not foresee how strongly Chinese expectations and customary practices would influence the transfer process.

The relationship between a foreign company and its Chinese employees is also shaped by Chinese custom. Chinese employees expect a foreign company to look after them in a total sense. A common saying about the state-owned enterprises was: 'The factory is my home; therefore, what belongs to the factory belongs to me.' To counteract this belief, Western managers have had to exercise strict control over assets and address an avalanche of petty theft. Chinese staff also place high expectations on the foreign company for personal and family benefits: housing, medical, retirement, education, travel, opportunities for promotion and income. They turn the relationship with the company into a moral issue with concomitant disillusionment if the company fails their expectations. This is a different philosophy from the capitalist enterprise's 'we are here to make a profit'. Both sides have had to deal with these different expectations.

The boss–subordinate relationship reflects the whole style of power relationships in Chinese society: directive from above with punitive discipline for the disobedient. In return for direction and the boss taking responsibility in decision-making, the subordinate will not infringe upon the leader's territory. The disciplinary father figure, present but distant, seems to be the most successful model. Of course, this runs counter to all the current Western theory and practice on workplace relationships: participatory, democratic and with a large margin for the exercise of individual initiative. Taiwanese companies know better the traditional power relationships between boss and subordinate and apply it in their companies.

Making the assumption from this directive boss–obedient employee model that Chinese employees are dependent and compliant is far from the truth. In some cases, employees have rioted and blockaded factories over redundancy, benefit and promotion issues. In other cases they have sabotaged Western management systems, actively or through indifference. A Western executive's inability to control the workforce leads to chaotic work practices, low productivity and a company that is effectively out of control. This is the great danger of applying Western management principles without considering the local context.

Official power

Government law-making has been unpredictable and the local bureaucracy neither impartial nor distant. The principle of local benefit dominates administrative decision-making. Officials have discretion over the issuing of licences and permits, customs clearances and taxation. They formulate and administer rules and regulations, and have the discretion whether or not to enforce administrative and court judgments in commercial disputes. Decision-making based on black letter laws and regulations is not clear and transparent. Unlike in most Western democracies, the power of Chinese officials transcends the purely administrative.

Western executives have found China not to be an administrative whole, but a nominally united country with strong local loyalties. They must deal with a multiplicity of local regulations and taxes, as well as highly protectionist and competitive behaviour towards other localities. Using expertise or products from other areas of China is vehemently discouraged. Marketing into another locality is made equally difficult by that locality's protectionist policies.

Commercial realities

Risk of all types has been high because China is a developing country without the huge infrastructure base of the advanced Western economies. The unexpected often catches Western executives unprepared. Risk minimisation concerning power, water supply and transport has been an essential lesson for Western executives.

Although China has maintained a high credit rating with international risk management agencies due to sovereign guarantees undertaken by the government, companies operating in China's market who are unprotected by sovereign guarantees, find debt a serious management problem.

Court judgments to recover debt cannot be enforced in many cases because Chinese businesses move money into other accounts. A long tradition is for businesses to keep two or three sets of accounts. This helps them to avoid tax and to keep information on the business within a trusted circle. Confidentiality among associates is further reinforced by the close association of officials with business in state-owned, collective and private enterprises. The tightness of this official–business linkage is reinforced by an official's inadequate public sector salary which is mightily improved by the profits from business. Trust is built on personal intimacy not law. Foreigners can be easily excluded from such personal networks, but they can also learn from the Chinese how to build relations with officials that benefit their business. They also learn when to apply a strict commercial basis to transactions to minimise accounts receivable.

Although many of the characteristics of Chinese business derive from the socialist period, they are uncannily reminiscent of Chinese business before 1949, when business and bureaucracy were intermixed—sometimes to the detriment of business and at other times to its advantage (see the BAT story in Chapter 2)—and when collusive arrangements by guilds and chambers of commerce shaped business life. How far China goes towards an international business environment is open to question, although it is certainly being pressured in this direction by the international business community.

At present a posting to China is a challenging assignment for Western executives, at once stimulating and frustrating. Western companies, in the main, persist in China with varying degrees of success and there are always new entrants to the market. Executives deal with the daily challenges as best they can, and how some individuals have met these challenges has been the subject of this book. They've told me about the China game, and what the rules of that game would seem to be.

Bibliography

Adams, Douglas and Carwardine, Mark 1991 *Last Chance to See* Pan Books Ltd, London

Atkinson, David 1998 Interviews for a university assignment, University of Ballarat

Baum, Julian 1999 'Hedging its bets' *Far Eastern Economic Review* vol. 162, no. 12, p. 16

Beijing Review 1999 *http://www.china.org.cn/bjreview/99jan/bjr99–3-3.html*

Brick, Jean 1991 *China: A Handbook of Intercultural Communication* Macquarie University, Sydney

Brodie, Patrick 1990 *Crescent over Cathay: China and ICI, 1898–1956* Oxford University Press, Hong Kong

Bruun, Ole 1993 *Business and Bureaucracy in a Chinese City* University of California Press, Berkeley

Chan, Wing-tsit 1969 *A Source Book in Chinese Philosophy* Princeton University Press, Princeton

Chang, Chung-li 1955 *The Chinese Gentry. Studies on their Role in 19th Century Society* University of Washington Press, Seattle

Child, John 1991 'A foreign perspective on management in China' *International Journal of Human Resource Management* vol. 2, no. 1, pp. 93–107

China Statistical Yearbook 1997 China Statistical Publishing House, Beijing

Cochran, Sherman 1980 *Big Business in China. Sino-Foreign Rivalry in the Cigarette Industry* Harvard University Press, Cambridge, MA

Cooper, Thomas T. 1871 *Travels of a Pioneer of Commerce in Pigtails and Petticoats* John Murray, London

Corne, Peter 1997 *Foreign Investment in China. The Administrative Legal System* Hong Kong University Press, Hong Kong

Crow, Carl 1937 *Four Hundred Million Customers*, Hamish Hamilton, London

Dolven, Ben 1999 'Wounded pride' *Far Eastern Economic Review* vol. 162, no. 27, p. 73

Fallon, Maura 1997 'Human resource operations in China' *China Practical Staff Employment Manual* ed. T. Frow, Pearson Professional, Hong Kong

Fukuyama, Francis 1996 *Trust: The Social Virtues and the Creation of Prosperity* Penguin Books, London

Goodman, Bryna 1995 *Native Place, City and Nation. Regional Networks and Identities in Shanghai, 1853–1937* University of California Press, Berkeley

Hall, Edward T. 1976 *Beyond Culture* Anchor Press, New York

Hansen, Valerie 1995 *Negotiating Daily Life in Traditional China* Yale University Press, New Haven

Hao, Yen-p'ing 1970 *The Compradore in 19th Century China: Bridge between East and West* Harvard University Press, Cambridge, MA

Harris, David 1997 *High Tide* Wakefield Press, Adelaide

Hoon-Halbauer, Sing Keow 1996 *Management of Sino-Foreign Joint Ventures* Lund University Press, Lund

Hou, Chi-ming 1965 *Foreign Investment and Economic Development in China 1840–1937* Harvard University Press, Cambridge MA

Huai-nan Tzu, 9:1a, 6b–7a. De Bary, W.T., Chan, W.T. and Watson, B. 1960 *Sources of Chinese Tradition* Columbia University Press, New York

Jiang, Xiaoli 1998 Interview in Tianjin

Killing, J. Peter 1983 *Strategies for Joint Venture Success* Croom Helm, London

Kleinman, Arthur 1988 *The Illness Narratives: Suffering, Healing and the Human Condition* Basic Books, New York

Kurain, George Thomas 1998 *Fitzroy Dearborn Book of World Rankings* Fitzroy Dearborn Publishers, Chicago

Kwong, Julia 1997 *The Political Economy of Corruption in China* M.E. Sharpe, Armonk

Lattimore, Owen 1990 *China Memoirs. Chiang Kai-shek and the*

War Against Japan compiled by Fujiko Isono, University of Tokyo Press, Tokyo

Leung, Yuen-sang 1997 *The Shanghai Taotai. Linkage Man in a Changing Society, 1843–90* University of Hawaii Press, Honolulu

Lin, Yutang 1939 *My Country and My People* rev. ed., William Heinemann Ltd, London

Liu, Kwang-ching 1962 *Anglo-American Steamship Rivalry in China 1862–1874* Harvard University Press, Cambridge, MA

Liu, Yia-ling 1992 'Reform from below: The private economy and local politics in the rural industrialization of Wenzhou' *The China Quarterly* no. 130, June, pp. 293–316

Liu, Zhenyun 1994 *The Corridors of Power* Chinese Literature Press, Beijing

MacGowan, D.J. 1886 'On Chinese guilds and chambers of commerce and trade unions' *Journal of the North Branch of the Royal Asiatic Society of Great Britain and Ireland,* vol. 21

MacPherson, K.L. and Yearley, C.K. 1987 'The 2 1/2 % margin: Britain's Shanghai traders and China's resilience in the face of commercial penetration' *Journal of Oriental Studies* vol. 25, no. 2

Mann, Susan 1987 *Local Merchants and the Chinese Bureaucracy 1750–1950* Stanford University Press, Stanford

Nee, Victor 1992 'Organizational dynamics of market transition: Hybrid forms, property rights, and mixed economy in China' *Administrative Science Quarterly* vol. 37, pp. 1–27

Orton, Jane 1997 'They give me jobs to do. The experience of young Chinese in Australian–Chinese joint ventures' *China Update, Newsletter of the Australia China Business Council* no. 5, November, p. 2

Parris, Kristen 1993 'Local initiative and national reform: The Wenzhou model of development' *The China Quarterly* no. 134, June, pp. 242–63

Rabe, John 1998 *The Good German of Nanking. The Diaries of John Rabe,* ed. E. Wickert, Little, Brown & Co., London

Rowe, William T. 1984 *Hankow: Commerce and Society in a Chinese City 1796–1889* Stanford University Press, Stanford

Silin, Robert H. 1976 *Leadership and Values: The Organisation of Large-scale Taiwanese Enterprises* Harvard University Press, Cambridge, MA

Tang, Yun Wei 1995 *Doing Business in China—The Environment for Joint Ventures* Price Waterhouse/Australia–China Chamber of Commerce and Industry, Melbourne

Transparency International and Dr Johann Graf Lambsdorff 1998 *http://www.transparency.de/*

United States–China Business Council surveys 1995 quoted in 'Feeling upbeat' *China Business Review* May–June, p. 39

——1996 confidential survey

——1998 quoted in 'Secrets of the supply chain' *China Business Review* September–October, p. 14

Upton, David and Seet, Richard 1994 *Pacific Dunlop China (A): Beijing* Case Study N9-695-029, Harvard Business School, Cambridge, MA

Wank, David L. 1996 'The institutional process of market clientelism: Guanxi and private business in a south China city' *The China Quarterly* no. 150, June, pp. 820–37

Ward, Edward 1969 *Number One Boy* Michael Joseph, London

Wong, C.P.W., Heady, C. and Woo, W.T. 1995 *Fiscal Management and Economic Reform in the People's Republic of China* Oxford University Press, Hong Kong

Worm, Verner 1997 *Vikings and Mandarins: Sino–Scandinavian Business Co-operation in Cross-cultural Settings* Handelschojskolens Forlag, Copenhagen

Yan, Yunxiang 1996 *The Flow of Gifts: Reciprocity and Social Networks in a Chinese Village* Stanford University Press, Stanford

Yates, Frank J. and Lee, Ju-Whei 1996 'Chinese decision-making' *The Handbook of Chinese Psychology* ed. M.H. Bond, Oxford University Press, Hong Kong

Ying, S. and Dong, H. 1991 'A study of the applicable laws in administrative reconsideration' in 'The administrative litigation law of the PRC: Changing relationship between the courts and administrative agencies in China' ed. P.B. Potter *Chinese Law and Government* vol. 24, no. 3, pp. 54–6

Young, Linda 1994 *Cross-talk and Culture in Sino-American Communication* Cambridge University Press, Cambridge

Young, Susan 1995 *Private Business and Economic Reform in China* M.E. Sharpe, Armonk

Zhu, Xinmin 1996 'International business-oriented development of personal connections in China' paper given at *Cross Cultural Management Conference*, Hong Kong Baptist University, August

Index